JOURNEY TO JERUSALEM

Celebrating and Teaching the Life of Jesus

BOYD LIEN

Published by Abingdon Press
Nashville

JOURNEY TO JERUSALEM:
Celebrating and Teaching the Life of Jesus

Copyright © 1988 by Abingdon Press

This book is printed on acid-free paper.

Library of Congress Cataloging-in-Publication Data

Lien, Boyd. 1943-
    Journey to Jerusalem: celebrating and teaching the life of Jesus
    / Boyd Lien.
        p.   cm.—(A Griggs educational resource)
    ISBN 0-687-20593-X (pbk. : alk. paper)
    1. Jesus Christ—Biography. 2. Christian education—Textbooks—
Presbyterian. 3. Christian biography—Palestine. I. Title.
BT307.L54   1988
232.9'01'07—dc19   88-919
                                                                           CIP

BOOK DESIGN BY JOHN ROBINSON

All scripture quotations, unless otherwise noted, are from the *Good News Bible,* the Bible in Today's
English Version. Copyright © American Bible Society, 1976. Used by permission.

Those noted RSV are from the Revised Standard Version of the Bible, copyrighted 1946, 1952, © 1971,
1973 by the Division of Christian Education of the National Council of the Churches of Christ in the
U.S.A., and are used by permission.

The section "Prayers on My Journey" on pages 74-82 is designed to be duplicated and used as a journal
by each "traveler."

Manufactured by the Parthenon Press at
Nashville, Tennessee, United States of America

To Jerry,
a traveling companion
and guide on my journey

CONTENTS

WELCOME TO THE JOURNEY

For me, few earthly delights compare with reading travel literature and planning trips. I get engrossed in every brochure, advertisement, guidebook, and train schedule that comes my way. Just reading a trip's itinerary sets my mind racing to imagine the people, scenery, and surprises that await the traveler. Anticipating a future trip floods my mind with pictures and my body with adrenalin. Therefore, it's no accident that I have combined my enthusiasm for travel with my commitment to Christian education by designing, leading, and now publishing this *Journey to Jerusalem.*

Eight years ago, to celebrate Epiphany, Lent, and Easter, our midweek Junior Fellowship group of the Third United Presbyterian Church in New Castle, Pennsylvania, made the first journey to Jerusalem. Using the language of travel, our community of faith was organized into passport-carrying travelers, sojourners, and pilgrims. Learning centers became *locales;* teachers/leaders were called *traveling companions;* the directions were provided as an *itinerary;* background information became the *tour guide;* and the schedule, of course, was known as the *timetable.*

Our initial gathering remains a vivid memory for me. As the children and adults entered the classroom, they were greeted with colorful posters, pictures, and maps placed on walls and dividers. Pillows were on the floor; a record player was all set for use; a table was laden with wood scraps; and many other areas of the room called out to be discovered and enjoyed. We began by gathering everyone together to talk about the exciting possibilities of this new style of learning adventure, one in which each of us was free to travel about and be responsible for our own learning. In three months, we had followed Jesus on his journey from the stable in Bethlehem to the eastern hills of Jerusalem and the road to Emmaus.

Since that initial, wonderful experience, I have had the opportunity to lead two other major Journey to Jerusalem events, in addition to leading numerous workshops on the theme. At Central Presbyterian Church in Eugene, Oregon, we celebrated Lent with an all-church Journey to Jerusalem for six Sunday mornings following the worship service. Individual classes were cancelled in order that our entire church family could gather on the journey. Images from those Sunday mornings are vivid. When people leaving worship reached the fellowship hall, they discovered a table of passports, walls and dividers labeled with both familiar and strange names, and tables stocked with various craft materials. We even provided a stop on the journey called "the Oasis" in order to incorporate our coffee fellowship into the journey. In a matter of minutes, the room was buzzing as 225 people traveled about, passports in hand, eager to discover and experience everything. Six Sundays later, when we celebrated

Jesus' resurrection, we did so with a greater understanding of the meaning of his life and ministry, his journey to Jerusalem.

Most recently, at Memorial Drive Presbyterian Church in Houston, Texas, we celebrated Palm Sunday with an all-church Journey to Jerusalem. In order to focus on Holy Week, only the seven Bethany to Emmaus locales were used. I'll never forget the enthusiasm of one of our young children, who insisted that his mother join him in doing *all* the activities at every locale before he would eat supper! (A light supper was served.)

Note that each of these events involved a different community of faith, a different time schedule, and a different physical setting—and all of them were successful! The experiences at Central and Memorial Drive was so successful that in time a Journey to Bethlehem to celebrate Advent and Christmas and a Journey to Rome to celebrate Pentecost and the continuing work of the Holy Spirit followed. Yet, as different as the three Journey to Jerusalem experiences were, they had much in common.

First there was an eagerness among the travelers to become involved in all the experiences of the journey. This was generated by providing interesting and worthwhile activities at the locales and was kindled by a few enthusiastic people who worked to get everyone involved. Second, there was an openness and a willingness to share with one another by reading, creating, or just talking. This was helped along by intentionally teaming up mixed ages at the locales as often as possible. We worked hard to build a community. Third, there was a desire, which was often expressed, to clarify Jesus' life by putting the various events in order. This desire gave momentum and propelled people through the journey. Fourth, there developed an increased appreciation of the idea of *life journey*. Each one of us is in on a journey, and experiencing the journey as well as the destination is God's gift. In the deepest sense, this Journey to Jerusalem is not just a historical travelogue, but a call to examine our faith journey as followers of Jesus Christ and to take hope in God's future.

Because of my experiences in creating and leading this journey, I have written this guide with the conviction that this format will work in many situations, among diverse communities of faith, within varying timetables. I am also convinced that the many benefits of travel will be yours as well—renewal, refreshment, and recommitment to life's continuing journey. Let this guide serve as an imaginative beginning for your own creativity.

Have a good trip! *Bon voyage! Gute Reise!*

Boyd Lien

How to Plan Your Journey

Determine a Timetable

The Journey to Jerusalem program was originally designed for fourteen one-hour sessions on Wednesday afternoons. When repeated, it was offered on six Sunday mornings following worship. Most recently, it was adapted for a two-hour event on the afternoon of Palm Sunday.

In other words, numerous timetables are possible for this journey. The schedule will be determined by each church's needs, existing programs, and special opportunities. Even though this journey has been designed for an extended period of time, it can be adapted to almost any timetable—a Sunday morning all-church series, a Sunday morning church school class, a midweek program, church family nights, a single all-church event, or a vacation church school. You will need to write your own ticket and plan a timetable that will meet your goals.

Consider the following suggestions as alternative ways to make your Journey to Jerusalem.

Timetable 1—A Lenten Series on Sunday Mornings for the Entire Church

In order to make this happen, invite all the individual classes that normally meet on Sunday morning to participate together in this special gathering. To ensure extensive participation, recruit each class to be responsible for one portion of the event.

Lent, the six Sundays preceding Easter, is an ideal time to follow Jesus to Jerusalem. Consider setting up the locales in the following order:

Week 1......... Bethlehem, Nazareth 1, Jordan River, Nazareth 2, Sea of Galilee
Week 2......... Nazareth 1, Jordan River, Nazareth 2, Sea of Galilee, Bethsaida
Week 3......... Sea of Galilee, Bethsaida, Capernaum, Caesarea Philippi, Jericho
Week 4......... Capernaum, Caesarea Philippi, Jericho, Bethany, Jerusalem: The Temple
Week 5......... Bethany, Jerusalem: The Temple, Upper Room, Gethsemane, Golgotha
Week 6......... Jerusalem: Upper Room, Gethsemane, Golgotha, Empty Tomb, Emmaus

Timetable 2—Sunday Morning Church School

Using the Journey to Jerusalem program in a Sunday morning church school provides the opportunity to spend more time at each locale and thus experience the itinerary in greater depth. It also makes it possible to bring in other teaching materials, such as films, songs and records, to amplify the experiences at each of the locales.

For churches using the lectionary in worship and education, the journey is perfectly compatible to the seasons of Epiphany and Lent—the scriptural story covers Jesus' baptism to his resurrection appearances. The flexibility of this journey format provides many ways to coordinate the worship themes, mission emphasis, and other educational activities of the congregation.

Timetable 3—A Midweek Program

Many churches provide midweek educational programs. Some are designed for children and youth and are held following school. Others, designed for all ages, are held in the early evening. The midweek setting offers many opportunities to expand the activities and to enrich the experiences. For instance, if participation in a choir is a part of the midweek program, appropriate hymns and songs can be learned and sung as a part of the journey. Some advantages of a midweek journey are a more relaxed time frame, the possibility to use more of the church building, and easier recruitment of leadership.

Timetable 4—One All Church Event

It is possible, and appropriate, to scale down the journey for just one event of two or three hours. For Palm Sunday afternoon, we used just the Bethany to Emmaus locales and focused our journey on Holy Week. On other occasions, various locales could be drawn together to express other themes—for example: Evangelism, Discipleship, Prayer. The number of locales used at an event depends on the anticipated size of the group of travelers. Certain embellishments could be added, such as serving a light supper, gathering for a closing worship experience, and even inviting other churches to join in the enjoyment (and perhaps the preparation) of the journey.

Timetable 5—Vacation Church School

There are many reasons why vacation church school is an advantageous time for the journey.

1. In a vacation church school setting, it is easier to create a community of travelers by building in shared experiences for the entire group. Needless to say, this becomes a difficult task when large numbers of people make the journey.

2. More time can be given to the activities at each of the centers. A structured pace for the journey would serve to provide a more relaxed atmosphere for the travelers.

3. With five or ten straight days together, the journey really comes together as the events of Jesus' life come together.

4. In the group setting of a vacation church school, there is the possibility of singing and learning some of the great songs of our faith.

Therefore, let me offer some suggestions about adapting this material for vacation church school.

Suggestion 1

One successful model for vacation church school depends on three variations on a theme—music, crafts, and movies. The structure of each day consists of blocks of time given to discovering the theme for the day by singing about the theme, creating in response to the theme, and seeing a movie that further develops the theme. The schedule for the day might look like this:

9:30- 9:45	A time for gathering
9:45-10:15	Music
10:15-11:00	Crafts
11:00-11:45	Movies, recreation, treats
11:45-12:00	A time for sharing

This format is viable for the journey when traveling to the locales is offered during the time for crafts. In addition, it would mean that supplemental movies and music designed around the themes of the locales would need to be provided. This is just one possibility; let me suggest some others.

Suggestion 2

Make the journey a one-week (five day) vacation church school. It is then possible to concentrate on three locales each day. A two-week experience (ten days) means that many more experiences would need to be planned for the expanded time frame.

Suggestion 3

In order to provide for group building and mutual support, begin the journey with a time for gathering and close with a time for sharing. A daily schedule may look like this:

9:30- 9:45	A time for gathering
9:45-10:15	Locale 1
10:15-10:45	Locale 2

```
10:45-11:15   Locale 3
11:15-11:30   Refreshments at the Oasis
11:30-12:00   A time for sharing
```

Suggestion 4

Rather than open the locales to individual exploring and discovery, divide the children, youth, and adults into smaller tour groups of mixed ages. Assign a youth or adult the responsibility to be the traveling companion with each group.

. . . .Then. . . .

Suggestion 5

Issue a ticket each morning for the travel plans of each group. Design it to look like an airline ticket. For instance:

Names of Passengers _____

Itinerary	Date	Time
From: The Sea of Galilee To: Bethsaida	August 14	9:45 A.M.
From: Bethsaida To: Capernaum	August 14	10:15 A.M.
From: Capernaum To: Caesarea Philippi	August 14	10:45 A.M.

In order to stagger the groups, the ticket for other groups will direct them to start the journey at a different time and a different locale. It is not necessary to visit the locales in order. The order of the locales can be altered as long as the scope of the day is discussed during the closing time for sharing.

Suggestion 6

Spread the locales around the church in order to provide some distance between them and take advantage of a variety of settings. Besides, everyone enjoys a change of scenery.

Suggestion 7

You may wish to adjust the daily schedule in order to show a movie or filmstrip to the whole group. You may have audio-visuals from other curricula that can be used. Excellent resources are available.

Sing together! One weakness of the scattered locales is the difficulty in sharing music. Sing as you gather together and once again as you disperse. Needless to say, an abundance of music is available that expresses every aspect of Jesus' life and journey.

Above all, remember that this book is a collection of ideas and resources. Design educational experiences for your children, youth, and adults, using your unique setting and following your particular goals. God be with you! Godspeed!

Choose a Tour Director

The best title to give the person in charge who serves as the administrator and spark plug for the experience may be: tour director. In this learning center format, where those serving as teachers/leaders (traveling companions) are responsible for just a portion of the whole, it is crucial that one person has oversight of every aspect of the journey.

Choose a tour director who is excited by the vision of the total experience, willing and eager to take the risks, and confident about the journey's ultimate success. As in all traveling, this journey involves some risks. When space is opened up and people are encouraged to move about, there is risk that the travelers will not know what to do, that some may feel lost. When all ages are brought together, there is the risk that adults may feel that they are treated childishly and vice versa. The tour director must be someone who will risk gladly, not becoming impatient with people who appear to be just standing around or annoyed with those who seem to be racing through each activity. In my extensive experience with this learning center format, every event has been worth all the risks, and in fact exceeded all expectations. Energetic interaction between young and old takes place, mutual discoveries are made, wonderful surprises are shared, and the body of Christ is strengthened.

The tour director by no means does all the work, but serves to pull the event together. Numerous people share responsibilities in setting up and supplying each of the learning centers (locales). Thus recruitment focuses on specific short-term tasks. People could be recruited to set the scene for each locale by finding appropriate pictures, maps, and decorations. People are needed to gather together the supplies for each of the locales. Most of the work on this journey comes in preparing the locales, much like getting ready to take a trip or to give a party. Once the first travelers arrive and visit the locales, we all become traveling companions and the journey begins.

Select Traveling Companions

Since the atmosphere of the journey is one of shared responsibility among all ages, there are no teachers on this journey, only "traveling companions." A sensitivity to everyone's needs must constantly be nurtured among the travelers because at various points people will need to give one another assistance. Those who read will need to be aware of their opportunity to help the nonreaders. Those who eagerly take to crafts will need to keep an eye out for those travelers who need some encouragement. Even the children need to be aware of helping to loosen up the adults and inviting them to become more childlike!

In a few locales, it is desirable to have a resident teacher/leader to guide certain tasks. Those needs will be highlighted in the description of the locales. Select these specific traveling companions not only because of their gifts, but also because of their ease in working in this setting.

Design the Locales

The area of the church to be used for the journey needs to be imaginatively arranged into a setting of many separate learning centers. Use dividers, tables, and existing objects in the room—pianos, pillars, and so on—to divide the learning space. Pay close attention to the flow of traffic in order to avoid creating bottlenecks at the locales.

All locales will need dividers or walls on which to mount the pictures, directions (itinerary), and other teaching materials. Some locales will need electrical outlets. Since new locales are set up and taken down week by week, or day by day, the look of the room will be constantly changing.

The section *Setting the Scene* in the description of each locale will provide instructions for putting together the locale and will offer suggestions about helpful resources, such as pictures, charts, maps, and so on.

Create the Passport

During the journey, the passport serves to draw together the experience of visiting so many learning centers. Many people, when set free in a room full of learning centers, need direction and encouragement in order to get involved in the activities. Having a passport in hand provides some direction for the enjoyment of the journey.

Each locale has its own stamp, and the opportunity to stamp the passport comes only upon the completion of the activities (itinerary). Thus, following the event, the passport serves as a visual reminder of the journey.

Encourage those who have United States or foreign passports to bring them to share with the group. Each passport usually contains some interesting passport and visa stamps of the countries visited.

At the end of this section, you will find illustrations that may be duplicated and used in making your passports. Follow these simple instructions:

1. Use two 8½" x 11" sheets of white or colored paper
2. Cut the paper lengthways and fold over
3. Staple the fold

You should end up with a passport that is 4¼″ x 5½″ with three sheets of paper inside a cover.

Depending on the time frame of your journey, you may wish to embellish the passport. Simple personal information forms could be added to the inside front cover as well as instant photos taken of each traveler.

Passport Stamps

Create the stamps for the passports with Styrofoam and wood blocks. The Styrofoam containers used at many fast food restaurants for hamburgers, fish sandwiches, and so on are ideal; the thin Styrofoam is perfect for cutting and indenting. A small wooden block, like a child's block, is used as the base for the stamp. The steps for creating the stamps are as follows:

1. Using the designs from the page of backward passport stamps, found on the following pages as your guide, trace just the *shape* of the stamp on the Styrofoam with a pencil or straight pin.
2. Cut out the basic shape of the stamp from the Styrofoam, using a X-acto knife or razor blade.
3. Glue this shape to the block with white glue and let it dry.
4. Using the same design, trace the *design* on the Styrofoam with a sharp pencil or straight pin. By tracing the design right over the Styrofoam, you will be indenting the surface.
5. Use a pencil or straight pin to indent further the surface of the Styrofoam. Remember, the indented design will not pick up ink from the stamp pad and when printed will show up white.
6. Try out the stamp with an inked stamp pad. Use different colors of inked pads for some variety. Be aware that after having been stamped many times, the image will not be as sharp.

PASSPORT

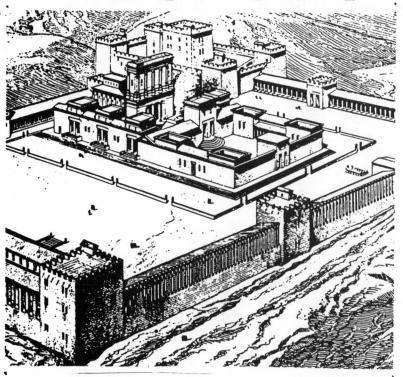

Name...

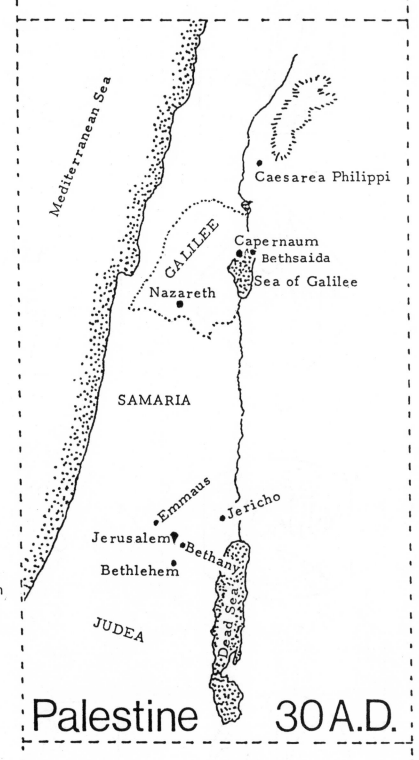

Mediterranean Sea

Caesarea Philippi

GALILEE

Capernaum
Bethsaida
Sea of Galilee

Nazareth

SAMARIA

Emmaus

Jericho

Jerusalem

Bethany

Bethlehem

JUDEA

Dead Sea

Palestine 30 A.D.

Use this map
of Palestine as
the center sheet
in the Passport
to Jerusalem.

Duplicate it on
an electronic
stencil, mimeograph
etc. Cut to size
along the vertical
dotted lines.
Fold and staple
in the fold with
the other sheets
and cover.

BACKWARD PASSPORT STAMPS

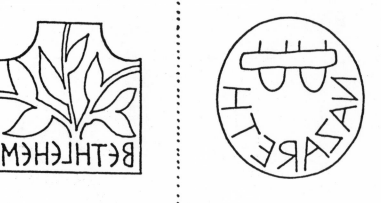

BACKWARD PASSPORT STAMPS

HOW TO USE THIS BOOK

ithin the description of each of the sixteen locales there are four sections:

Historical Notes.   This section reads like a travel guide and provides biblical documentation and archaeological evidence of the locale, while also noting its contemporary status.

Tour Guide.   The particular focus of the locale and the choice of readings and activities are explained. Some locales, such as *The Upper Room,* provide obvious choices of scripture and activities. Others, such as *Capernaum,* take on a new fascination because of discoveries made. The tour guide also tries to anticipate questions you may have about the suggested Itinerary.

Itinerary.   In keeping with the language appropriate to travel, the set of directions at each locale is called the itinerary. These directions are to be copied exactly as written and posted in the most prominent place at the locale. The language of the itinerary has been intentionally simplified in order to be understood by children as well as adults.

Setting the Scene.   Suggestions for posting the itinerary and decorating the locale are found here. In choosing the extent of the decorations, consider a number of factors: Will the locales stay up during the week, or will they need to be taken down and set up every week? Is there enough space available? Are people with time to decorate available? Also in this section is a complete checklist of the necessary supplies needed for supplying the locale.

The Historical Notes, Tour Guide, and Setting the Scene sections serve primarily as background information for the tour director and the person putting the locale together. If you think that the historical notes would enhance the enjoyment of the travelers, this section could also be posted as a part of the locale. Another possibility would be to print a small travel guide containing the historical notes either to go along with the passport or printed and bound within the passport.

A form, picture, or chart is provided in many locales. These camera ready originals can be reproduced in quantity on an offset press or photocopy machine.

How to Deal with Roadblocks, Detours, Travel Sickness, and Missed Connections

1. What do I do about the reluctance on the part of some adults to get involved?

Some adults may prefer to stand around and observe. The learning center format may be unfamiliar to them, and they may be puzzled about how to get involved. In most cases, offering a word of encouragement or a simple set of instructions will be enough to engage them—unless they really would rather stand around! I have discovered that stand-bys enjoy the experience just by taking it all in. An almost fool-proof way to get them involved is to give them a child as a partner.

Some youth may prefer to huddle together and not participate in the locales. Enlist their help in making the journey a success. Assigning each of them to a particular task may work wonders.

It is not crucial that everyone on the journey be involved at the same level of commitment and intensity. What is crucial is the complete acceptance of all travelers. Remember, educating in the Christian faith concerns nurturing a life-style rather than accumulating information.

2. What do I do with those who feel lost in the learning center setting and do not know what is expected?

The tour director and the traveling companions are crucial to the success of the journey. They need to keep an eye on the travelers and give guidance when appropriate. Since the passport leads the traveler through the journey, a traveling companion may be positioned at the passport table rather than just a stack of passports. The companion would be able to interpret the journey, answer questions, and offer a hearty *bon voyage!* Your work in putting together this journey is to make things look spontaneous. Remember, people learn through discovery, and serendipities are unplanned.

3. What do I do about those who do not want to do anything that's artsy-craftsy?

Since people learn in various ways, this journey provides activities that use all the senses—sight, touch, smell, taste, and sound. And since people learn in different ways, this journey provides a balance of left brain/right brain activities. Some travelers will choose to center on the readings, word studies, and writing assignments. Great! Others will put up with the reading just to get to the "fun stuff"—the craft activities. Trust the travelers to choose how they will most enjoy their visit to the locale. After all, learning will take place, even if the traveler does not want to color a stained-glass window!

4. What do I do about those who want to go directly to the crafts without doing the scripture reading?

Excellent question! First, make sure you provide enough Bibles at the locale to encourage using the Bible before plunging in. Second, be sure to encourage the readers to help non-readers. I have seen some wonderful things happen because of this. Third, don't be reluctant to say something to those who are not fully enjoying the locale. Fourth, think smorgasbord. You have prepared the menu and set the table, now it is up to the participants to eat a well balanced meal. Alas, some will only choose dessert! Fifth, if it gets out of line, provide a traveling companion at each locale to guide the progress of the travelers.

Sometimes the travelers will not follow the itinerary in order, but will return later to finish up. Remember, people do not learn in an orderly manner, but rather accumulate, put pieces together, make connections, and enjoy "aha" moments.

5. What do I do with people who speed through the activities to see how many they can finish?

First, I would suggest offering just a few locales at a time. Otherwise people will worry that they will never have the chance to complete everything. Second, I would try to link up someone who is racing through the activities with someone who needs help. For example, ask the speedy person to help a younger child with the reading or a craft activity. In doing so you, will give that person a gift: the opportunity to share.

Remember, as we teach we must also model the kingdom and set in motion the love, acceptance, compassion, and understanding of Jesus Christ.

6. What do I do when I feel hassled and harried about putting everything together?

You are not doing it right! Share the load. Ask for help. Delegate the responsibilities and graciously accept the results. The more people who are brought in to work on the journey, the more participants who will make the journey. Another discovery I have made is to depend on the group to take care of itself and expect some wonderful surprises. Remember, people learn when they are teaching. Sharing responsibilities is a gift of learning.

An Overview of the Journey

Locale	Scripture	Focus	Activity
Bethlehem	Luke 2:1-7	Jesus' Birth	Family Tree Name Tag
Nazareth: Jesus the Child	Luke 2:39-40	Jesus' Youth	Wood Cross Pendant
Jordan River	Mark 1:9-11 Matt. 28:16-20	Jesus Is Baptized	Baptism Banner
Nazareth: Jesus Begins His Ministry	Luke 4:16-30	Jesus' Ministry Begins	Scrolls
Sea of Galilee	Matt. 4:18-22	Jesus Calls Disciples	Fish Stained-Glass Window
Bethsaida	Luke 9:1-17 Matt. 25:31-46	Jesus Feeds the Hungry	Filmstrip Illumination
Capernaum	Mark 2:1-12	Jesus Heals the Sick	Interview: Healing Hands
Caesarea Philippi	Matt. 16:13-23	Who Is Jesus?	Picture Display Portraits
Jericho	Luke 10:25-37	Jesus Teaches	Storyteller Greeting Cards
Bethany	Luke 19:28-38	Jesus Enters Jerusalem	Matching Pictures Holy Week Puzzle
Jerusalem: The Temple	Matt. 21:12-17	Jesus in the the Temple	Film Coin Display
Jerusalem: Upper Room	Luke 22:14-20	Jesus Shares a Special Meal	Picture Display Communion Bread
Jerusalem: Gethsemane	Mark 14:32-50	Jesus Prays	Wall of Prayers Prayers on My Journey
Jerusalem: Golgotha	John 19:17-18	Jesus Dies	Discovery Tour Planting Seeds
Jerusalem: Empty Tomb	All Four Gospels	Jesus Lives!	Gospel Study Butterflies
Emmaus	Luke 24:13-35	Jesus Christ Is Risen Today	Songs of Easter

BETHLEHEM

Historical Notes

Our journey to Jerusalem, which will take us throughout Judea and Galilee, actually begins in Bethlehem, a small village six miles southwest of Jerusalem.

> When the angels went away from them back into heaven, the shepherds said to one another, "Let's go to Bethlehem and see this thing that has happened, which the Lord has told us."
> So they hurried off and found Mary and Joseph and saw the baby lying in the manger. . . .
> A week later, when the time came for the baby to be circumcised, he was named Jesus, the name which the angel had given him before he had been conceived. (Luke 2:15-16, 21)

Prior to the birth of Jesus, the importance of Bethlehem centered on the lives of Ruth, Jesse, and David. Bethlehem is the setting for most of Ruth's story. She is an important part of David's family tree. Jesse, David's father, made his home in Bethlehem. There Samuel anointed David as the future king of Israel (I Samuel 16:1-13). Jesse was soon associated with an important symbol for the coming Messiah. The prophet Isaiah declared that "The royal line of David is like a tree that has been cut down; but just as new branches sprout from a stump, so a new king will arise from among David's descendants" (Isaiah 11:1). God's Messiah was to be born into the family of David; in fact, Matthew begins his Gospel by showing Jesus' position in the family tree of David and Abraham.

Pilgrims have been visiting the birthplace of Jesus since the second century. Early tradition identified a specific cave as the actual birthplace. In A.D. 339 the first church was built by the Emperor Constantine over that cave. The present Church of the Nativity on that same sight dates from the time of the Emperor Justinian (A.D. 527–565). Bethlehem today is a disappointment for most visitors. The church, the tasteless adornments, the crowds, and the souvenir hawkers are a far cry from the lovely simplicity of the Christmas story; yet, in viewing the hills and fields around Bethlehem one is still able to imagine just how it was when Jesus was born.

Tour Guide

The focus of our visit to Bethlehem is on names—Jesus' name, the names on Jesus' family tree, and our names. Since this is the locale most people will visit first, it is the ideal place to make name tags. The creation of a name tag is linked to the meaning of our names, which in turn is linked to the meaning of Jesus' name.

Itinerary

Welcome to the journey! Our journey begins just six miles away in the small village of Bethlehem.

1. Read the story in Luke 2:1-7. Mary and Joseph journeyed from Nazareth, their home, to Bethlehem. Jesus was born in Bethlehem, in the city of King David. Jesus was a part of David's family tree.

It was important that he was named Jesus. Why? What does the name mean?

2. Read the story in Luke 1:26-33 or Matthew 1:18-23. Names are very important for the Jewish people. Every name has a meaning. In Jesus' family tree there are a number of important names which tell us something about the person.

3. Using the form "Jesus' Family Tree," discover what the name *Jesus* means. Then choose a name of one of Jesus' ancestors and discover what it means. Use one of the Bible dictionaries to find definitions; then write down the meanings.

4. Jesus was given a number of other names during his lifetime. Find the definition of the two names on Jesus' Family Tree and write down your discovery. Names are important; they tell us something about Jesus. Jesus lived up to his name!

5. Your name is important; it tells us something about you. Make a name tag to wear on the journey. In addition to writing your name, write down what your name means. Use a special dictionary of names to discover the meaning, unless you already know it.

6. Wear your name tag as our journey continues.

Setting the Scene

The following directions and suggestions will help you put together the locale and set the scene as we begin our journey in Bethlehem.

   1. Post the itinerary.
   2. Decorate the locale.

At the beginning of every journey, travelers are interested in knowing where they will be going and what they will be doing. Preview the entire journey by mounting a map of Israel on a wall or a divider. In some way highlight each of the stops on the journey—use signs, passport stamps, and so on—and then connect them by drawing a heavy line on the map or by stringing yarn to each city or by putting down small foot prints. You may want to display some pictures of the other locales and string yarn from the picture to the actual city on the map. Since the focus is on names, add interest by translating the names of the locales. Consider using just the translation in labeling the city and see if anyone can guess the actual name. Some locales and their translations are:

Bethlehem—house of bread
Nazareth—guard place, watchtower
Galilee—ring, circle, district
Bethsaida—house of the fisher
Capernaum—village of Nahum
Bethany—house of Ananiah
Jerusalem—foundation of Shalom
Gethsemane—oil vat
Golgotha—skull
Emmaus—warm wells

3. Supply the locale.

Checklist:
Bibles
"Jesus' Family Tree" form for each traveler
Pencils, pens
Bible dictionaries, name dictionaries

4. Set out passport stamp and stamp pad.

JESUS' FAMILY TREE

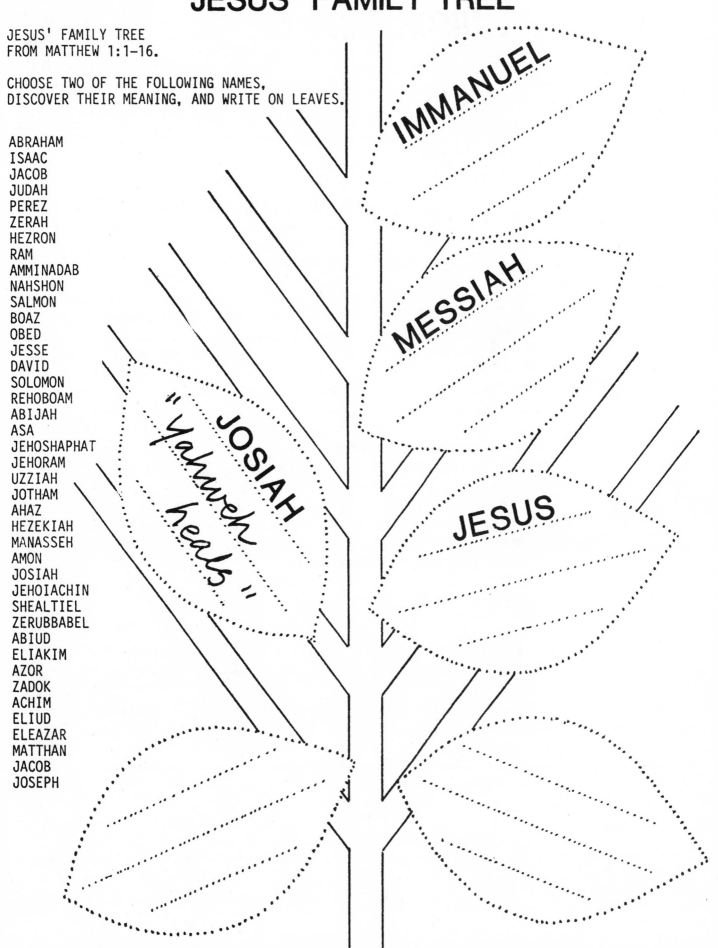

JESUS' FAMILY TREE
FROM MATTHEW 1:1–16.

CHOOSE TWO OF THE FOLLOWING NAMES,
DISCOVER THEIR MEANING, AND WRITE ON LEAVES.

ABRAHAM
ISAAC
JACOB
JUDAH
PEREZ
ZERAH
HEZRON
RAM
AMMINADAB
NAHSHON
SALMON
BOAZ
OBED
JESSE
DAVID
SOLOMON
REHOBOAM
ABIJAH
ASA
JEHOSHAPHAT
JEHORAM
UZZIAH
JOTHAM
AHAZ
HEZEKIAH
MANASSEH
AMON
JOSIAH
JEHOIACHIN
SHEALTIEL
ZERUBBABEL
ABIUD
ELIAKIM
AZOR
ZADOK
ACHIM
ELIUD
ELEAZAR
MATTHAN
JACOB
JOSEPH

IMMANUEL

MESSIAH

JOSIAH "Yahweh heals"

JESUS

NAZARETH: JESUS THE CHILD

Historical Notes

> When Joseph and Mary had finished doing all that was required by the law of the Lord, they returned to their home town of Nazareth in Galilee. The child grew and became strong; he was full of wisdom, and God's blessings were upon him. (Luke 2:39-40)

Nazareth, a small village in Galilee, was the home of Joseph, Mary, and Jesus. All the references to Nazareth in the Bible are found in the New Testament, and all are used in connection with Jesus, who is identified nineteen times as "Jesus of Nazareth." Mary was living in Nazareth when she received the announcement from the angel Gabriel (Luke 1:26). After Jesus' birth in Bethlehem, Joseph and Mary returned home to Nazareth to live (Luke 2:39-40). Other than one episode from his twelfth year, all our knowledge about Jesus between his birth and his baptism is contained in one verse: "The child became strong; he was full of wisdom, and God's blessings were upon him." We know that Joseph was a carpenter (Matthew 13:55) and that Jesus also learned the trade (Mark 6:3).

Today Nazareth is a city of 41,000 people and has the largest Christian population of any city in Israel. Today's visitor will see many churches and shrines that have been built throughout the centuries to commemorate the sacred events in the hometown of Jesus, Mary, and Joseph.

Tour Guide

This locale centers on Jesus the Carpenter, with particular emphasis on two wooden products: the yoke and the cross—two vivid visual images of discipleship.

In so many of his teachings, Jesus used an everyday object and transformed its meaning. Simple things were used to communicate simple, yet profound, truths.

For example, he taught about discipleship by using a yoke. Jesus certainly knew how one was made and perhaps had crafted many. But more important, he also knew that it was used for training animals to do the work and to ease the effort by sharing the load (at least with a double yoke). At this locale, the traveler is invited to consider the gracious invitation to put on the yoke of Christ.

When Jesus taught about discipleship on another occasion, he said, "If anyone wants to come with me . . . he must forget himself, carry his cross, and follow me" (Mark 8:34). The complete transformation of the cross was realized with Jesus' death on one and his ultimate resurrection victory. Today, with an Easter faith, we make this wooden object at this locale to constantly remind us of our call to be disciples. Later in our journey, at Golgotha, we will consider more fully the meaning of Jesus' cross.

Itinerary

Our journey has brought us to the village of Nazareth—the home of Mary, Joseph and Jesus.

1. Read about Jesus' boyhood in Luke 2:39-40. This account tells us almost all we know of Jesus' boyhood, other than that he became a carpenter like Joseph (Mark 6:3). As carpenters, Joseph and Jesus made many things out of wood, including yokes. Yokes were used to train animals to plow the land.

Later in his life, Jesus said to those who wanted to follow him and be his disciples, "Take my yoke and put it on you, and learn from me. . . . For the yoke I will give you is easy, and the load I will put on you is light" (Matthew 11:29-30). Jesus knew that loving God and loving others was not a burden but a joy. He promised a yoke that pulled an easy load.

2. To remember Jesus' youth in Joseph's carpentry shop in Nazareth, create something out of wood, using the wood, nails, glue, saw, and hammer you find here in Nazareth. When you have finished, leave what you made for other travelers to enjoy. Following today's journey, remember to pick it up and take it with you.

At another time, Jesus said to those who wanted to be his disciples, "If anyone wants to come with me . . . he must forget himself, carry his cross, and follow me" (Mark 8:34). Jesus knew that serving God and serving others was not a burden, but a joy. He promised a cross because his victory on the cross was a sign of hope and new life.

3. Create and wear a wooden cross to remember Jesus' life and our call to be his disciples.

Directions:
- Use one long and two short pieces of balsa wood to make the cross.
- Drill a hole through the top of the long piece and string a cord through.
- Glue the two short pieces on the long pieces to form a cross. Make sure you glue on the same side as the hole.
- Let it dry.
- Wear it and remember Jesus' love! Wear it and remember your call to share his love!

4. Stamp your passport!

Setting the Scene

The following directions and suggestions will help you put together the locale and set the scene as we visit Nazareth, Jesus' hometown.

1. Post the itinerary.

2. Decorate the locale. Excellent travel posters are available from the Israel Government Tourist Offices—Chicago, Houston, Los Angeles, Miami Beach, and New York. If unable to obtain posters directly, contact a local travel agency. In addition to the picture of Nazareth, create a display depicting the use of yokes on animals. If possible, let the travelers see and examine an actual wooden yoke.

For the wooden crosses, you will need to pre-cut the pieces of balsa wood and the lengths of macrame cord. Gather together scraps of wood in all shapes and sizes to set out on the table. Call on carpenters in your congregation to contribute wood scraps. Provide hammers, saws, nails, and so on within reason.

3. Supply the locale.

Checklist:

Bibles
Yoke display—pictures and so on.
Scraps of wood in all shapes and sizes
Nails, hammers, saws
White glue
Supplies for wooden crosses
    3″ pieces of ¼″ balsa wood
    1″ pieces of ¼″ balsa wood
    lengths of macrame cord for around the neck
    hand drill with a small bit (but large enough to get the cord through)

4. Set out passport stamp and stamp pad.

The Jordan River

Historical Notes

> Not long afterward Jesus came from Nazareth in the province of Galilee, and was baptized by John in the Jordan. (Mark 1:9)

Mark, the earliest of our Gospels, begins with the urgent message of John the Baptist, "I baptize you with water, but he will baptize you with the Holy Spirit" (Mark 1:8). When Jesus was baptized by John in the Jordan River, his actual journey to Jerusalem began.

As a major river in the country, the Jordan was the scene of many significant events in Israel's history. Jacob crossed it freely, but Moses died without crossing over to enter the Promised Land. Joshua and the people of Israel crossed over in triumph to occupy Canaan. Saul and David both crossed the Jordan by night to escape impending defeat. Elijah and Elisha both passed through waters that miraculously divided. Naaman was cured by the Jordan's water upon Elijah's command, and Elijah's axe head floated on his command. In the very same river, which was the scene of so many of God's mighty acts, Jesus was baptized.

In the years after his baptism, Jesus was never far from the Jordan River, ministering primarily in the towns around the Sea of Galilee.

Baptism marked both the beginning and the end of Jesus' ministry, for the final words of Matthew's Gospel are Jesus', "Go, then, to all peoples everywhere and make them my disciples: baptize them in the name of the Father, the Son, and the Holy Spirit" (Matthew 28:19).

Tour Guide

What else do Christians think of when they hear the name *Jordan River* other than baptism, especially Jesus' baptism? On our visit, we reflect on the biblical story by visually interpreting one aspect of it in the creation of a banner. The celebration of the sacrament of baptism is a wonderful occasion for displaying a ceremonial banner, especially one that is a community effort.

Itinerary

You are now standing on the banks of the Jordan River. The real beginning of Jesus' journey to Jerusalem began when Jesus came here to be baptized by John the Baptist.

1. Read the story in Mark 1:11.

2. Help us tell the story of Jesus' baptism by creating one square for our patchwork Baptism Banner.

Directions:
On one square of felt, design one of the following images from the story in the Bible or an image that you associate with baptism:
- Jesus
- John the Baptist
- The Jordan River
- Dove
- Hand
- Water
- A head
- Sandals

Leave the square you create to add to our banner.
Once all the squares have been designed _____ will sew them together in a patchwork banner. You may wish to make another square to take along with you as a reminder of Jesus' baptism.

Jesus, at the completion of his ministry, told his followers to baptize new disciples.

3. Read the story in Matthew 28:16-20. We continue to baptize people because of Jesus' command. For future baptisms in our church, we will display our special Baptism Banner.
How are people baptized in our church? Enjoy the slide show depicting some of the baptisms that have taken place in our church.

4. Stamp your passport!

Setting the Scene

The following directions and suggestions will help you put together the locale and set the scene as we gather at the river—the Jordan.
1. Post the itinerary. Print the itinerary on large sheets of paper or poster board.
32 Post in the most prominent location and decorate around it.

2. Decorate the locale. The spiritual "Roll, Jordan, Roll" makes the meandering river sound like a mighty rush of water. Actually, it's quite narrow and quiet. Many pictures of tranquil scenes of the river may be used. The *Reader's Digest Atlas of the Bible* has an interesting two page spread (pp. 178-79). Additional banners, created for celebrations and seasons, could be used to complete the decor. Pictures of water in all its uses—cleaning, replenishing, growing, nourishing, purifying, and so on—would make an intriguing display.

One way to draw a connection between the ancient story and our contemporary practice is to prepare a slide show or picture display of actual baptisms in your church. A photograph using a telephoto lens and fast speed film will not disturb many people during a service of worship. Obviously this will take some long range planning, especially if baptisms are infrequent.

Enlist a quilter/seamstress to sew the banner pieces together and finish it off.

3. Supply the locale.

Checklist:
  Bibles
  Squares of felt in various colors
  Other felt—large pieces, scraps, and so on
  Yarn, ribbon
  White glue
  Pencils
  Scissors

4. Set out passport stamp and stamp pad.

NAZARETH: JESUS BEGINS HIS MINISTRY

Historical Notes

Then Jesus went to Nazareth, where he had been brought up, and on the Sabbath he went as usual to the synagogue. He stood up to read the Scriptures and was handed the book of the prophet Isaiah. He unrolled the scroll and found the place where it is written,

> "The Spirit of the Lord is upon
>   me,
>   because he has chosen me to
>   bring good news to the
>   poor,
> He has sent me to proclaim
>   liberty to the captives
>   and recovery of sight to the
>   blind,
> to set free the oppressed
>   and announce that the time
>   has come
>   when the Lord will save his
>   people."

(Luke 4:16-19)

When Jesus began his public ministry, he returned home to Nazareth and preached in the synagogue. His sermon on that occasion is best understood as the inaugural proclamation for his entire ministry, for in identifying himself with Isaiah 61:1-2, Jesus provided the context for all his subsequent actions.

Other than when it is used to identify Jesus—Jesus of Nazareth—the town does not appear again in the New Testament. Its insignificance is evident in Nathanael's remark, "Can anything good come from Nazareth?" (John 1:46).

Nazareth today is anything but insignificant. As a major Christian city in Israel, it is visited by thousands of pilgrims each year. Indeed, Nazareth is so linked with Christianity that the modern Hebrew word for Christians is derived from the name of the town—*Notzrim.*

Tour Guide

In order to emphasize the impact of Jesus' reading from the scroll of Isaiah, the activity at this locale is putting together a scroll and copying the words of the prophet. This provides not only an opportunity to focus on those powerful words of Isaiah, but also serves as an introduction to the Hebrew language and the use of scrolls. It will provide many insights to those eager to understand the earliest formation of the scriptures.

A simple scroll is created by attaching a long length of paper to two craft sticks. The words of Isaiah are copied from the six phrases, in Hebrew and in English, included in this book. I have made the Hebrew letters as simple as possible for copying. People have many unique ways of handwriting this fascinating alphabet!

This locale will be enriched by having a resident traveling companion who knows enough about the Hebrew language to amplify the activity—such as identifying words, phrases, and the names of God and pointing out various letters of the alphabet, vowel markings, and so on.

Itinerary

What did Jesus say and do when he began his ministry of preaching, teaching, and healing? For the answers, we have returned to Nazareth.

1. Read the story of Jesus' return to his home, in Luke 4:16-30. At that time, the scriptures were written on scrolls—not in books—and the words were Hebrew, not English. Jesus read the words of Isaiah that were written in Hebrew on the scroll.

2. Make an Isaiah scroll to remember your journey to Nazareth.

Directions:
- You will need two sticks and one long sheet of paper.
- Glue the sticks to each side of the paper.
- Use the Hebrew pages of Isaiah 61:1-2 and copy one or all of the six phrases on your scroll in Hebrew and in English. Remember: Hebrew reads backwards! That means you should probably copy it from right to left.
- Roll up the scroll. To read, just unroll it!

3. Stamp your passport!

Setting the Scene

The following directions and suggestions will help you put together the locale and set the scene as we worship at the synagogue in Nazareth.

1. Post the itinerary. Instead of writing the itinerary on poster boards, it would be in keeping with the theme for you to write it instead on a large sheet of paper. Roll up the ends to make it look like an unrolled scroll.

2. Decorate the locale. Appropriate decorations for this stop on the journey would be pictures of a synagogue and pictures of scrolls. For instance, volume twelve of *The Interpreter's Bible* has an excellent selection of photographs of historical scrolls (pp. 628-44).

Search through your picture files of old curricula for other scroll representations. In addition, it would be interesting to display a contemporary Hebrew Bible.

3. Supply the locale. Reproduce a few copies of the two pages of Hebrew phrases. The number needed will depend on the number of travelers using the locale at one time.

Checklist:
Bibles
Sticks for scrolls (look for craft sticks in an art supply store or hobby shop)
Long sheets of paper for scrolls
Hebrew/English phrases to copy
Pencils, crayons, marking pens, glue

4. Set out passport stamp and stamp pad.

THE SOVEREIGN LORD HAS FILLED ME WITH HIS SPIRIT

TO BRING GOOD NEWS TO THE POOR

HE HAS SENT ME TO HEAL THE BROKENHEARTED

TO ANNOUNCE RELEASE TO THE CAPTIVES

TO PROCLAIM THAT THE TIME HAS COME

TO COMFORT ALL WHO MOURN

The Sea of Galilee

Historical Notes

Following his baptism, "Jesus returned from the Jordan full of the Holy Spirit and was led by the Spirit into the desert" (Luke 4:1). Just as the site of Jesus' baptism is uncertain, so is the site of his wilderness sojourn. Tradition has placed the scene of Jesus' wrestling with temptation in the barren hills around Jericho.

Upon his return from the wilderness, Jesus journeyed north to Galilee and chose his disciples. Matthew recorded the scene in this way:

> As Jesus walked along the shore of Lake Galilee, he saw two brothers who were fishermen, Simon (called Peter) and his brother, Andrew, catching fish in the lake with a net. Jesus said to them, "Come with me, and I will teach you to catch men." At once they left their nets and went with him.
> He went on and saw two other brothers, James and John, the sons of Zebedee. They were in their boat with their father Zebedee, getting their nets ready. Jesus called them, and at once they left the boat and their father, and went with him. (Matthew 4:18-22)

How appropriate that Jesus used the language of fishing to call these new disciples! Since they depended on fishing for their livelihood, he used an image from their everyday struggle to call them to a vision of the new struggle.

Fishing has taken place in the Sea of Galilee for centuries. An early name for that body of water was the Lake of Chinnereth, named after a nearby town. The word *Chinnereth* means "lyre," and either referred to the shape of the town or to the shape of the lake. Other names in the New Testament, referring to the same body of water, are Lake Gennesaret (Luke 5:1) and the Sea of Tiberius (John 6:1).

F. F. Bruce has written that

> the modern visitor finds it difficult to envisage the thriving towns which surrounded the lake in Jesus' time. The lake teemed with fish, which provided a living for many of the inhabitants of those towns. The fish they caught were not only sent to other parts of Palestine and Transjordan, but was salted and exported to other lands. Magdala, between Capernaum and Tiberius, was given the Greek name of Tarichaeae, because of the salt fish (tarichos in Greek) which it exported. (F. F. Bruce, *Jesus and Paul: Places They Knew,* p. 21)

Today the visitor to the Sea of Galilee finds a lake much larger than expected, yet as beautiful and peaceful as hoped for.

Tour Guide

Jonah's is not the only great fish story in the scriptures! It is fascinating to follow the image of the fish through Jesus' life and teaching. Fish were crucial when Jesus fed five thousand people (Matthew 14:17). Jesus compared the kingdom of heaven to a net filled with fish (Matthew 13:47-50). Jesus revealed himself to Peter through the great catch of fish (Luke 5:1-11). After his resurrection, Jesus joined his disciples to eat fish (Luke 24:42). And where would John 21:1-14 be without fish?

Our activities at this locale first examine the variety of fish stories and then focus attention on the major fish symbol—IXOYE—Jesus Christ God Son Savior.

Itinerary

Welcome to the shores of the Sea of Galilee, a large inland sea (lake) twelve miles long and eight miles wide. Jesus came to the Sea of Galilee to call disciples to share his ministry.

1. Read the story in Matthew 4:18-22. When Jesus told his disciples that they would be just like fishermen in sharing the good news about God, he wished for every person to know God, to love God and to serve God. Fish are often an important part of stories about Jesus.

2. Read one of the following stories:
   Matthew 14:3-21—Jesus fed five thousand people with two fish and five loaves.
   Matthew 13:47-50—Jesus taught that the kingdom of heaven is like a net full of fish.
   Luke 24:36-43—Jesus ate fish with his disciples on Easter Sunday.
   Later, after his resurrection, the fish was used as a symbol of Jesus.

3. Look at the Greek words at the left and their English translation on the right.

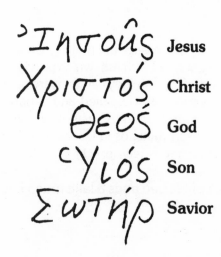

Ἰησοῦς Jesus

Χριστός Christ

Θεός God

Υἱός Son

Σωτήρ Savior

When the first letters of the five Greek words are put together, they spell IXOYE, which is the Greek word for "fish."

4. To remember your journey to the Sea of Galilee, create a fish stained-glass window. In the window, you will find:
- a large fish
- the Greek word for fish/the names of Jesus
- a net reminding us of the story Jesus told in Matthew 13:47-50
- five loaves of bread and two fish, which fed the crowd of five thousand people
- the empty cross; after his resurrection, Jesus ate fish with his disciples

Directions for making your window:
- Color your window with crayons or liquid markers.
- Turn the paper over and rub the back with vegetable oil. Use just enough to soak through the paper. Rub off all the extra oil.
- Place the paper within the picture frame and tape or staple it in.
- Hang it up on or near a window as a joyful reminder of your visit to the Sea of Galilee.

Remember your invitation to be like a fisherman in sharing the good news about God's love.

5. Stamp your passport!

Setting the Scene

The following directions and suggestions will help you put together the locale and set the scene as we walk along the shore of the Sea of Galilee.

1. Post the itinerary. The itinerary could be written on poster boards or on sheets of paper in the shape of a fish or the shape of a boat.

2. Decorate the locale. Since we are on the sea, let your imagination run wild in depicting life along the Sea of Galilee—boats, fishermen, nets, fish, and so on. Why not bring in a boat, fishing nets, and fishing gear? Travel posters of the Sea of Galilee portray a locale almost untouched through the centuries.

Reproduce copies of the fish stained-glass window for the travelers. Paper frames, which finish off the window and also keep oil off the fingers, should be cut in advance. Use two 8½" x 11" pieces of construction paper. Leave a one inch border all around and cut out the center. The traveler will then place the completed design between the two pieces of the frame and tape or staple it in.

3. Supply the locale.

Checklist:
Bibles
Copies of the fish stained-glass window
Paper frames for the window (cut these out beforehand)
Crayons, liquid markers

Vegetable oil
Paper towels
Tape, staples, and stapler for securing the paper frame

4. Set out passport stamp and stamp pad.

BETHSAIDA

Historical Notes

Bethsaida, a fishing village on the north shore of the Sea of Galilee, was the scene of Jesus' miraculous feeding of five thousand people.

> The apostles came back and told Jesus everything they had done. He took them with him, and they went off by themselves to a town named Bethsaida. . . .
>
> . . . Jesus said to them, "You yourselves give them something to eat."
>
> They answered, "All we have are five loaves and two fish. Do you want us to go and buy food for this whole crowd?" (There were about five thousand men there.)
>
> Jesus said to his disciples, "Make the people sit down in groups of about fifty each."
>
> After the disciples had done so, Jesus took the five loaves and two fish, looked up to heaven, thanked God for them, broke them, and gave them to the disciples to distribute to the people. They all ate and had enough, and the disciples took up twelve baskets of what was left over. Luke 9:10, 13-17)

Bethsaida was also the scene of Jesus' miraculous healing of the blind man (Mark 8:22-26). Yet, Jesus' anger was directed at Bethsaida, for even though he had performed those mighty works there, the citizens had refused to believe (Luke 10:13). Notice that he instructed the man he healed, "Don't go back into the village" (Mark 8:26). Bethsaida is also identified as the home of three disciples: Philip, Andrew, and Peter (John 1:44).

Today, the location of ancient Bethsaida remains a mystery. Even though scholars place it on the north shore of the Sea of Galilee, some indicate that it was west of the Jordan, others east. Add to this the suggestion that there may have been two Bethsaidas, for the name means "a house or place of fishing." For the modern pilgrim in the Holy Land, the traditional site of Tagba, west of Capernaum, offers a modern church containing an ancient loaves and fishes mosaic to support its claim to being the authentic locale of the miracle.

Tour Guide

Our focus in the feeding of the five thousand is not on the miraculous aspect of Jesus' action but the reason for his compassionate response. Jesus fed the people because he knew they were hungry.

44

This is an ideal place to consider Jesus' parable of the sheep and the goats,

Matthew 25:31-46, a story not linked to a particular locale, but one certainly connected to Jesus' ministry of compassion. This focus is stressed in two biblical readings, a contemporary retelling of the story, and in an activity designed to evoke a response in the traveler.

The theme of feeding the poor, expressed by Joel in the filmstrip discussed below, can be developed by considering our own responsibilities to a hungry world. Rather than cite one specific learning activity, I would encourage you to relate those hunger programs your church is already involved in locally, nationally, and worldwide. Each of the denominational hunger programs have interpretative materials and education resources available.

Itinerary

On the north shore of Galilee lies the village of Bethsaida. We have traveled far to see and hear Jesus of Nazareth. In fact, a large crowd has gathered because they know Jesus will be here.

1. Choose *one* of the following:

- See and hear the story by viewing the filmstrip *The Boy Who Gave His Lunch Away*. Play the record with the filmstrip and use the book to follow along if you wish.
- Read the story in John 6:1-14 or Luke 9:10-17.

During his life Jesus always responded to people's needs. Here at Bethsaida, Jesus was concerned that the people were hungry. Jesus was so concerned about people helping others that later in his ministry he told his disciples a story.

2. Read the story in Matthew 25:31-46. How do we respond to a hungry world? Jesus tells us in his story. We must care for our brothers and sisters; we must do it for him.

3. To remember Jesus' words, decorate an illumination of his words. Color it as you wish and put it up somewhere at home. Put it somewhere where you'll see it—on the refrigerator door, inside the front door, next to the phone, and so on—to remind you always.

4. Stamp your passport!

Setting the Scene

The following directions and suggestions will help you put together the locale and set the scene as we find a place to sit on the crowded hillside near the village of Bethsaida.

1. Post the itinerary.

2. Decorate the locale. Since no one has identified the site of Bethsaida, it may be best to display teaching pictures of Jesus feeding the multitude. Additional decorating will be determined if you choose to expand the theme of feeding a hungry world.

3. Supply the locale. Reproduce sufficient quantities of the illumination of Matthew 25 for the travelers. Paint pens, especially gold and silver, are ideal for painting the illuminations.

Checklist:
  Bibles
  Arch filmstrip *The Boy Who Gave His Lunch Away*
  Copies of the Arch book of the same title
  Filmstrip projector
  Record player
  Copies of illumination of Matthew 25
  Paint pens, marking pens, and so on
  Hunger program materials (optional)

4. Set out passport stamp and stamp pad.

I was hungry and you fed me,

I thirsty and you gave me a drink;

I was a stranger and you received me in your homes,

I naked and you clothed me; I was sick and you took care of me,

in prison and you visited me.

Whenever You did this for one of the least of these brothers and sisters of mine, you did it for Me!

Matthew 25:35-36,40

CAPERNAUM

Historical Notes

When Jesus heard that John had been put in prison, he went away to Galilee. He did not stay in Nazareth, but went to live in Capernaum, a town by Lake Galilee, in the territory of Zebulun and Naphtali. (Matthew 4:12-13)

For Jesus, being "at home" meant being in Capernaum (Mark 2:1). For that reason, it is one of the most important locales in Jesus' Galilean ministry.

In fact, Capernaum and Jesus' healing ministry are almost synonymous. Whenever Capernaum is mentioned, it is usually in relation to a healing of one of the many people who sought out Jesus there to be healed. Capernaum is the setting for the healing of the centurion's servant (Matthew 8:5-13), a man with an unclean spirit (Mark 1:21-28), the government official's son (John 4:46), Peter's mother-in-law (Matthew 8:14-17), and the paralytic who was sent down through the roof (Mark 2:1-12).

In Jesus' day, Capernaum was an important and prosperous city, no doubt due to its location on the trade routes. In our day, it has been difficult to locate ancient Capernaum. Two sites on the northwest shore of the Sea of Galilee compete for designation as the city. The archaeological site Tell Hum (Arabic) is now identified as ancient Capernaum. Today's visitors view a fascinating mile of ruins, including substantial remains of a third-century synagogue that may stand on the site of the synagogue of Jesus' day.

Tour Guide

Capernaum provides a convincing reason for learning to use a Bible concordance. What one discovers by checking *Capernaum* in the concordance is that *Capernaum* and *healing stories* go hand in hand. For this reason, Capernaum is the perfect location for looking at Jesus as a healer of bodies, hearts, and minds. The contemporary aspect of visiting ancient Capernaum comes in considering how God continues today to heal those sick in body, heart, and mind. We see healing offered all around us. Who else could it be but God at work? Whose hands are they but Christ's? Use of the interview form will bring travelers together for sharing and will release some wonderful testimonies.

Itinerary

We are in Capernaum, a city on the north shore of the Sea of Galilee. We are here because Jesus is home. Whenever he is home, people who are sick travel to see him. How did Jesus respond to those who were sick and suffering? We read that in the city of Capernaum Jesus "healed many who were sick with various diseases" (Mark 1:34). Wherever Jesus went, he healed the sick, gave sight to the blind, and cured people of their diseases.

Sometimes Jesus healed by speaking. Many times Jesus healed by putting his hands on a person.

1. Read two or more of the following stories to discover the times Jesus offered hands of healing.

Matthew 8:1-14
Matthew 9:18-19
Mark 7:31-37
Luke 4:38-41
Luke 5:12-16
Luke 13:10-14

2. Answer these questions on the Capernaum Interview Form about the two stories you read.

What was the need?
How did Jesus respond?
How did the healed person respond?

God continues to heal people today. Jesus' ministry of love continues in the healing hands other people offer. Through healing, mending, curing, researching, caring, helping, praying, embracing, and sharing, healing hands are offered by doctors, nurses, counselors, friends, family, and strangers. Among your traveling companions, people have stories to tell about the healing, caring, and compassion they have known.

3. Use a clip board and Capernaum Interview Form to see what you can discover about God's continuing care. Trace hands of healing to discover ways people pray, help, care, and heal.

4. Stamp your passport!

Setting the Scene

The following directions and suggestions will help you put together the locale and set the scene as we visit Capernaum, a beautiful town right on the Sea of Galilee.

1. Post the itinerary.

2. Decorate the locale. Since Capernaum is one of those cities that has remained relatively ancient, today's traveler sees a close approximation of what Jesus must have known. Therefore, photos and posters of Capernaum should be used in setting the scene. It would be in keeping with the theme if a variety of pictures depicting Jesus as a healer were also displayed. Duplicate enough Capernaum Interview Forms for travelers and provide a supply of clipboards. An inexpensive clipboard can be made by cutting pieces of cardboard or masonite (10″ x 13″ or so) and adding medium-sized clips purchased at a stationery store.

3. Supply the locale.

Checklist:

Bibles
Copies of "Capernaum Interview Form"
Clipboards
Pencils, pens

4. Set out passport stamp and stamp pad.

Capernaum Interview Form

Hands of Healing

Choose two of the following stories and answer these questions:

	What was the need?	How did Jesus respond?	How did the healed person respond?
Matthew 8:1-14			
Matthew 9:18-19			
Mark 6:1-6			
Mark 7:31-37			
Luke 4:38-41			
Luke 5:12-16			
Luke 13:10-13			

Capernaum Interview Form

Hands of Healing

Trace the hand of someone who has been in the hospital.

Write the person's answers to these questions inside their hand print.
—Who in the hospital helped with your healing?
—Who gave you care?
—Who offered hands of healing?

Trace the hand of someone who has been cared for by another person when sick.

Write the person's answers to these questions inside the hand print.
—Who reached out with hands of healing?
—How did you feel when you were cared for in this way?

Trace the hand of someone who has taken a meal to someone who was sick or lonely or needed other help.

Write the person's answers to these questions inside the hand print.
—How did you feel when you cared for another person in this way?
—Why did you offer hands of healing?

Trace the hand of someone who has prayed for another person who was sick.

Write the person's answers to these questions inside the hand print.
—What did you pray?
—What does it mean to you to offer hands of healing in prayer?

Trace the hand of someone who has known that he or she was being prayed for when sick.

Write the person's answers to this question inside the hand print.
—How did you feel, knowing people were offering hands of healing in prayer for you?

Caesarea Philippi

Historical Notes

Jesus went to the territory near the town of Caesarea Philippi, where he asked his disciples, "Who do people say the Son of Man is?"

"Some say John the Baptist," they answered. "Others say Elijah, while others say Jeremiah or some other prophet."

"What about you?" he asked them. "Who do you say that I am?"

Simon Peter answered, "You are the Messiah, the Son of the living God." (Matthew 16:13-16)

Caesarea Philippi has been recorded in our gospels, and thus remembered, solely because it was the setting for Peter's confession of faith. It was one of the "villages near Caesarea Philippi" (Mark 8:27), located at the foot of Mount Hermon, that was the setting for Jesus' transfiguration following Peter's confession.

Over the centuries, these villages and towns have had numerous names. Today the name of Caesarea Philippi is Banias, reflecting the ancient Canaanite name Paneas. The tourist sites are Greek and Roman temple ruins, rather than anything specifically related to Jesus.

Tour Guide

Each one of us carries an image of God in our mind. Invite anyone to describe the image or draw the picture of God in his or her mind and you will discover that many people share a common picture—an old, gray-haired man sitting on a throne in the clouds. In a similar, but more diverse, way, each one of us holds a picture of Jesus in our mind. What does Jesus look like to you? What is he doing? Is his expression friendly? Is he somber or laughing? Is his image focused or blurry? Encouraging people to share their pictures of Jesus is one way to respond to Jesus' question, "Who do you say that I am?" In addition, the opportunity to view a great variety of artistic depictions of Jesus helps us not only to see the images of others, but also to realize that each era, each culture, and each person represents Jesus as one of them.

Itinerary

We have reached the territory of Caesarea Philippi in the far north of Palestine. Jesus and his disciples have withdrawn from Galilee for a short time.

During Jesus' travels around Caesarea Philippi, Peter and the disciples made an important discovery.

1. Post the story in Matthew 16:13-23. Jesus asked his friends, "Who do you say that I am?" Peter answered, "You are the Messiah, the Son of the living God."

"Who do *you* say that I am?" Over the centuries, people have answered that question in their own way. Artists especially have tried to interpret who Jesus is by drawing or painting or sculpting the way they picture him.

2. Look closely at the display of pictures that show the many ways Jesus has been understood and expressed by artists. Then respond to the questions written below some of the pictures. Attach your comments to the display so that other travelers will benefit from your thoughts and feelings. Jesus asks *us*, "Who do you say that I am?"

3. You also have the opportunity to respond to Jesus' question. You may wish to respond visually by drawing, painting, or sculpting how you picture Jesus. Or you may wish to respond by writing an "I believe" statement. When you have finished, attach your visual or written offering to our display.

4. Stamp your passport!

Setting the Scene

The following directions and suggestions will help you put together the locale and set the scene as we head north to Caesarea Philippi.

1. Post the itinerary. Keep the posted itinerary simple in design so that it does not compete with the display of pictures of Jesus. Watch for a visual overload!

2. Decorate the locale. This locale is best decorated with wall-to-wall pictures of Jesus, especially portraits. In addition to what you are able to gather from your teaching picture file, an excellent source is *The Faces of Jesus* by Frederick Buechner. You may want to buy two copies so that you can cut them up and mount various pages on the display. Another excellent book is *He Was One of Us* by the Dutch artist Rien Poortvliet. Make sure you seize the opportunity to have this display embrace artistic expressions from around the world. Just imagine the ways different cultures have depicted him! Many travelers will be interested in knowing who painted the picture or sculpted the statue, so add that information to the display.

Select some of the portraits to be "major portraits" and provide space around those pictures for the travelers to attach their comments and responses. Consider adding the following questions, or others like them, under each of the selected portraits:

—When you look at this picture of Jesus, what kind of person do you see?
—How do you feel when you see this picture of Jesus?
—What words do you think best describe this picture of Jesus?
—What do you think the artist wanted to communicate about Jesus?

For those who wish to paint, draw, or sculpt, provide the necessary media—paint, brushes, markers, pencils, paper, clay, and so on.

For those who wish to write, provide pieces of paper that are headed "I believe. . . ." It may be helpful to have a few of these already written out and posted on the display. Offer your personal response and also consider adding short statements from historical confessions of faith.

3. Supply the locale.

Checklist:
Bibles
A display of portraits of Jesus
Pencils, markers, brushes, paint, clay, and so on for visual expression
Paper for written responses to pictures
Paper for "I believe" statements

4. Set out passport stamp and stamp pad.

JERICHO

Historical Notes

A teacher of the Law came up and tried to trap Jesus. "Teacher," he asked, "What must I do to receive eternal life?"

Jesus answered him, "What do the Scriptures say? How do you interpret them?"

The man answered, "Love the Lord your God with all your heart, with all your soul, with all your strength, and with all your mind"; and 'Love your neighbor as you love yourself.' "

"You are right," Jesus replied; "Do this and you will live."

But the teacher of the Law wanted to justify himself, so he asked Jesus, "Who is my neighbor?"

Jesus answered him, "There was once a man who was going down from Jerusalem to Jericho. . . ." (Luke 10:25-30)

Jericho, the oldest continuously inhabited city in the world, is a city with an amazing history. Recent archaeological digs have uncovered at least three different sites that were occupied over the centuries—beginning perhaps eleven thousand years ago! The last great city was actually inhabited three hundred years before Moses.

In Jesus' day, as the winter capital of the kingdom, Jericho was a city of great wealth and great poverty, a home for both merchants and beggars. We read that Jesus, in passing through Jericho, healed the blind beggar Bartimaeus (Mark 10:46-52) as well as enjoyed the hospitality of the wealthy Zacchaeus (Luke 19:1-10). In his parable of the good Samaritan, Jesus described an incident that took place on the ancient road that descended for fifteen miles from Jerusalem to Jericho through the Wadi Qilt.

Today the Jericho of Jesus' time—a site called Tulul Abu el-'Alayiq—is separated from the Old Testament Jericho by a distance of two miles. The more ancient Jericho to the north is a mound called Tell es-Sulton, a site near Elisha's fountain. The oasis of Jericho is truly unforgettable.

Tour Guide

A common theme for these stories of Jesus and Jericho could be described as "the unlikely recipients of God's love." Even the story of the good Samaritan—our focus here in Jericho—emphasizes this theme. In all of these encounters, it was the most unlikely person who either received love and caring or who provided it. Rather than heal the powerful who were sick, Jesus healed the blind beggar. Rather than dine with the powerful Pharisees, Jesus shared a meal with a short, unpopular tax collector. And rather than receiving care from a priest or a Levite along the road, the beaten traveler found compassion in a Samaritan!

Jesus' story of the good Samaritan begins with a question, one that has become our own: "Who is my neighbor?" Jesus helps us discover the answer —among the most unlikely people.

Itinerary

Welcome travelers! Our destination is Jericho—home of Bartimaeus, a blind man healed by Jesus, and Zacchaeus, a tax collector friend of Jesus.

1. Gather around as _____ shares with us a story Jesus told about another traveler who was on the way to Jericho.

2. Who are our neighbors? Here at our church we have many neighbors. Look at our display of pictures and posters of our neighbors from around our church and around the world.

3. Send a greeting card to one of our neighbors. You may either add your name and a message to one of the large cards or create a card of your own. These greeting cards are one way we can share our love and concern for our neighbors. Many more opportunities will be given to each of us every day in the journey we are making.

4. Stamp your passport!

Setting the Scene

The following directions and suggestions will help you put together the locale and set the scene as we enter the ancient oasis in the desert, Jericho.
1. Post the itinerary.
2. Decorate the locale.

Excellent photographs of Jericho exist in biblical archaeology books. Kathleen Kenyon, the great Bible archaeologist, spent years excavating Jericho. Her record is entitled *Digging Up Jericho*. Another source for photographs is the monthly magazine *The Biblical Archaeologist*.

In addition to depicting the actual look of Jericho, it will be necessary to create a display of "neighbors." Be imaginative! You can add photographs of your church's homebound members, students away at college, service personnel, those studying overseas, foreign missionaries, and persons from the community around your church. Include photographs that portray a wide diversity of cultures, settings, and life-styles.

57

Many variations are possible with the greeting cards. If you pre-address your cards, it is possible to connect the envelope and the card on the table to a photograph with a piece of yarn. Post a world map and string a piece of yarn from the card and addressed envelope to the country of its destination. If you do not pre-address your cards, addresses will need to be a prominent part of your display, perhaps right over the appropriate photo. Provide postage stamps for the letters in order to reinforce the fact that these cards will actually be sent.

3. Supply the locale.

Checklist:
Bibles
Paper, envelopes, postage stamps
Marking pens, paint pens, tissue paper, and glue
Rubber stamps, potato prints, stickers, and so on
Be imaginative!

4. Set out passport stamp and stamp pad.

BETHANY

Historical Notes

Thus far, our journey has followed Jesus throughout Galilee, the center of his ministry for three years. Now it is time to journey south to Judea, to Jerusalem. This turning point in Jesus' ministry is told in just one sentence: "As the time drew near when Jesus would be taken up to heaven, he made up his mind and set out on his way to Jerusalem" (Luke 9:51).

In such a way, Luke both depicts Jesus' determination to journey to Jerusalem and signals the reader to anticipate the conclusion of Jesus' ministry.

Jesus entered Jerusalem with the knowledge that his ministry would initially bring confrontation and, ultimately, completion.

Jesus' home and headquarters during his week in Jerusalem was Bethany, the home of Lazarus, the home of his friends Lazarus, Mary, and Martha, just two miles east of Jerusalem (Matthew 21:17).

> Six days before the Passover, Jesus went to Bethany, the home of Lazarus, the man he had raised from death. . . .
>
> A large number of people heard that Jesus was in Bethany, so they went there, not only because of Jesus but also to see Lazarus, whom Jesus had raised from death. (John 12:1,9)

It was in Bethany that Jesus raised Lazarus from the dead (John 11:44); visited with Mary and Martha (Luke 10:38-42); supped with Simon the leper (Mark 14:3-9); and departed from his disciples after his resurrection (Luke 24:50-51).

Today the Moslem name for Bethany is "El-Azariyeh," named after Lazarus, who is considered a saint by the Moslem inhabitants. Among the tourist attractions are the tomb of Lazarus, the Franciscan Church of St. Lazarus, and archaeological relics from ancient churches built on the holy sites.

Tour Guide

Our visit to Bethany serves as a preparation for the events of Jesus' final week in Jerusalem. The major purpose of the activities is to assist the traveler in putting together the many events of Holy Week. Another concern is to provide a devotional resource to guide the traveler through the celebration of Holy Week, when all the pieces of the puzzle do indeed come together.

To meet the first concern, one simple activity is matching the day of the week with the appropriate scene from Jesus' life. To address the second concern, a

Holy Week Puzzle is designed as a devotional guide to be used in the home during Holy Week itself.

Itinerary

Praise God!
> God bless him who comes in the name of the Lord!
>> God bless the coming kingdom of King David, our father!
>>> Praise be to God!

Greetings such as these were shouted for Jesus as he rode into the city of Jerusalem.

1. Read the story of the first Palm Sunday in Mark 11:1-10. When Jesus entered Jerusalem, his earthly ministry was brought to completion. Here in Bethany you will be introduced to Jesus' final week.

2. In order to preview the events of Holy Week, match the pictures of Jesus in Jerusalem with the day of the week on which each event took place.

3. Begin to prepare for the celebration of Easter by creating a Holy Week Puzzle. _____ will guide you in putting this picture of Jesus together.
You will need two parts for the puzzles:

—a colored background sheet with the suggested Bible readings.
—a white puzzle-piece sheet

Begin your puzzle here at Bethany. Cut out the puzzle piece for Palm Sunday. Read the suggested Bible verses. Glue the piece in place. Color it now or later.

4. Stamp your passport!

Setting the Scene

The following directions and suggestions will help you put together the locale and set the scene as we enter the village of Bethany, just east of Jerusalem.
1. Post the itinerary.
2. Decorate the locale. Don't scour your picture files or travel literature for a picture of Bethany, either ancient or modern! Modern Bethany is just buildings crowding a very busy highway. One needs an active imagination to picture the ancient village that was once in that location. Instead, spend time putting together a vivid depiction of Palm Sunday, using pictures of Jesus riding into the city, palm branches, and so on. Since the locale is a preparation for Jerusalem, it would be appropriate to show a panoramic view of the city and indicate the location of Bethany—maybe even indicating Jesus' possible Palm Sunday route. There is an excellent drawing of this nature in the *Reader's Digest Atlas of*

the Bible: An Illustrated Guide to the Holy Land (pp. 184-85). You might invite someone who has been to Israel to share pictures. A continuous slide show may be of interest. There is an abundance of ideas; use your resources and creativity.

There are also various ways to put together the matching pictures activity. One way would be to mount the pictures on poster board and label the days of the week on a table top. Then, the traveling companion can hand each traveler the stack of pictures and instruct the person to place the pictures on the table in the correct order. (This is a locale where a resident traveling companion is needed). Another way is to mount a set of eight hooks on a room divider, wall board, and so on for hanging the set of pictures. Write the day of the week above each hook.

Mount eight pictures individually on poster boards and punch a hole at the top of each one so they can be placed and hung on the hooks. However you set up the matching pictures, you will need to sort through your pictures files, magazines, and curricula for the appropriate pictures to use. The theme of the picture for each day is as follows:

Palm Sunday—Jesus enters Jerusalem
Monday—Jesus drives the money-changers out of the Temple
Tuesday—Jesus teaches the crowds in the Temple or city streets
Wednesday—Jesus teaches his disciples
Maundy Thursday—Jesus shares the Passover meal with his disciples
Good Friday—Jesus upon the cross
Holy Saturday—Sad disciples in front of the stone-blocked tomb
Easter Sunday—The resurrected Christ!

(Only the Gospel of Mark indicates that Jesus confronted those in the Temple on Monday. Tuesday and Wednesday are interchangeable; we do not know what specifically happened on those days, but from the scriptures we see that Jesus spent his time teaching the crowds and giving final instructions to his disciples.)

3. Supply the locale.

    Checklist:
      Bibles
      Wall room divider, board with eight hooks, or table top with eight days of the week indicated
      Eight pictures/paintings of Jesus during Holy Week
      Copies of the "Holy Week Puzzle" (colored background sheet and white puzzle-piece sheet)
      Scissors
      Glue
      Crayons, colored pencils, marking pens, and so on

4. Set out passport stamp and stamp pad.

Holy Week Puzzle

"I came that they may have life, and have it abundantly."

He *"laid him in a tomb which had been hewn out of the rock; and he rolled a stone against the door of the tomb."*

Read MARK 15:42-47

"So they took Jesus, and he went out, bearing his own cross, to the place called the place of a skull....There they crucified him."

Read JOHN 19:17-30

"Do not be amazed; you seek Jesus of Nazareth, who was crucified. He has risen, he is not here; see the place where they laid him."

Read MARK 16:1-8

"Hosanna to the Son of David! Blessed is he who comes in the name of the Lord! Hosanna in the highest!"

Read MATTHEW 21:1-9

"Truly, I say to you, as you did it to one of the least of these my brethren, you did it to me."

Read MATTHEW 25:31-46

"Father, if thou art willing, remove this cup from me; neverthe-less not my will, but thine be done."

Read Luke 22:39-46

"You shall love the Lord your God with all your heart, and with all your soul, and with all your mind, and with all your strength.... You shall love your neighbor as yourself."

Read MARK 12:28-31

"He took bread, and when he had given thanks he broke it and gave it to them, saying, 'This is my body.'"

Read LUKE 22:7-20 and JOHN 13:1-15

"I am the Alpha and Omega, the first and the last, the beginning and the end."

Read REVELATION 22:12-13

"I am the vine, you are the branches."

Read JOHN 15:1-12

Palm Sunday   Monday   Tuesday   Wednesday

Place these first three pieces so that the small † is at the top of the design.

Maundy Thursday

Good Friday   Saturday   Easter Sunday   Easter Week

JERUSALEM: THE TEMPLE

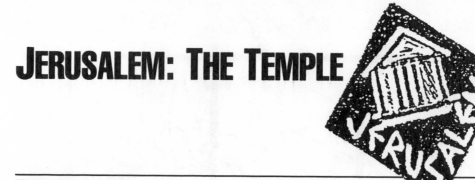

Historical Notes

When Jesus arrived in Jerusalem on Palm Sunday, he went to the Temple with his disciples.

> Jesus went into the Temple and drove out all those who were buying and selling there. He overturned the tables of the money-changers and the stools of those who sold pigeons, and said to them, "It is written in the Scriptures that God said, 'My Temple will be called a house of prayer.' But you are making it a hideout for thieves!"
>
> The blind and the crippled came to him in the Temple, and he healed them. (Matthew 21:12-14)

This was not Jesus' first appearance in the Temple. Four occasions are specifically indicated in the Gospels; other times are simply suggested. As an infant, he was taken to the Temple for the ceremony of purification (Luke 2:22-38). At age twelve, during a visit for the Passover festival, he discussed the faith with the Jewish teachers (Luke 2:41-51). Twice, John tells us, Jesus visited the Temple, during the Feast of Tabernacles (John 7:14–8:58) and the Feast of Dedication (John 10:22-39).

The Temple that Jesus entered was actually the third reconstruction on that sacred site. Even before the first Temple, the site was revered as Mount Moriah, the place where Abraham made an altar to sacrifice Isaac (Genesis 22:2). The first Temple, the magnificent creation of King Solomon, stood for three hundred fifty years until it was destroyed by the Babylonians in 587 B.C. The second Temple, created by Zerubbabel, was built following the return of the exiles in 516 B.C. and stood for four hundred years. The Temple Jesus knew, the Temple of Herod, had been extensively restored and enlarged in 20 B.C. It stood barely ninety years before being destroyed by the Romans in A.D. 70.

Whereas the entire Temple complex was holy, as one progressed east to west it became even more sacred, so restrictions were maintained. The setting for Jesus' throwing out the moneychangers was in the large area of the Temple, called the "Outer Court." It was the only part of the Temple open to Gentiles. The next restricted area, past the Beautiful gate, was designated the "Women's Court." Women gathered, but could proceed no further into the Temple complex. This was the location of the Temple treasury, where Jesus saw the poor woman give her coins. Next came the "court of Israel," which was set aside for male Jewish worshipers. Finally, the "Priest's Court" was the sanctuary itself and included the porch, the holy place, and the Holy of Holies.

Today just sections of the Temple of Jesus' day are to be seen in Jerusalem. The most extensive, the western wall of the Temple of Herod—the "Wailing Wall"—is both a holy place and a national symbol for the Jewish people.

Tour Guide

In our visit to the Temple, we focus our attention not on Jesus' anger or on the moneychangers or on prayer (see Gethsemane), but on offerings and gratitude—specifically, two offering stories from Jesus' days in the Temple. The first episode concerns a trap set by the chief priests:

> But Jesus saw through their trick and said to them, "Show me a silver coin. Whose face and name are these on it?"
>
> "The Emperor's," they answered.
>
> So Jesus said, "Well, then, pay to the Emperor what belongs to the Emperor, and pay to God what belongs to God." (Luke 20:23-25)

The other episode concerns the offering of a poor widow:

> Jesus looked around and saw rich men dropping their gifts in the Temple treasury, and he also saw a very poor widow dropping in two little copper coins. He said, "I tell you that this poor widow put in more than all the others. For the others offered their gifts from what they had to spare of their riches; but she, poor as she is, gave all she had to live on." (Luke 21:1-2)

Although separated in the Gospel of Luke by just twenty verses, the two stories are variations on the same theme: gratitude to God.

Itinerary

When Jesus entered Jerusalem, he went to the Temple and chased out those who were more interested in buying and selling things than in praying to and worshiping God.

1. Read the story in Matthew 21:12-17. During the next few days, Jesus taught and healed people in the Temple.

One day he saw a poor woman putting money in the temple offering plate and was deeply moved by how much she shared.

2. To see and hear the story, watch the movie *Show-Off*. In this film, the artist, Annie Vallotton, retells Jesus' story about a woman who gave all she had. _____ will show us the movie.

3. View our display of ancient coins. Notice the pictures on the coins—faces, animals, plants, numbers, designs. One day when he was at the Temple, Jesus was shown one of these coins.

4. Read the story in Luke 20:21-26. Jesus answered their trick question by having them look at the picture on the coin, "Pay to the Emperor what belongs to the Emperor."

But what do you think Jesus meant when he said, "Pay to God what belongs to God"?

5. Respond to this question by designing a coin. For this special coin, draw a picture that shows something that "belongs to God."

6. Stamp your passport!

Setting the Scene

The following directions and suggestions will help you put together the locale and set the scene as we enter the Temple in Jerusalem.

1. Post the itinerary.

2. Decorate the locale. With some imagination, the learning area could be much more than a wall and a table. Create a quiet setting by enclosing the space and maybe even adding simple pillars made of cardboard, rug rolls, or papier mâché. All the illustrations of the Temple you may find are only educated guesses of what it may have looked like.

For the coin display, you will discover excellent pictures of coins in *The Interpreter's Bible,* volume 1, pp. 157-64; *New Testament Illustrations,* pp. 90-92; and the *Reader's Digest Atlas of the Bible,* pp. 24-25. Perhaps you will uncover a numismatist in your congregation who would assume the responsibility of gathering together an appropriate display. Inquire also at a coin dealer's shop for possible loans of some ancient coins. Since many cheap replicas of these coins exist, it is not necessary to find the real thing.

This is a locale that requires a traveling companion to show the movie, rewind the movie, show the movie, and so on. Obviously, for the viewing of the movie, you will need to provide a dark area.

3. Supply the locale.

Checklist:
Bibles
Materials for coin display
Coin patterns
Pencils, marking pens, and so on for designing coins
Film: *Show Off* (this Story Line film may be purchased or rented from the American Bible Society, 1865 Broadway, New York, NY 10023)
Film projector

4. Set out passport stamp and stamp pad.

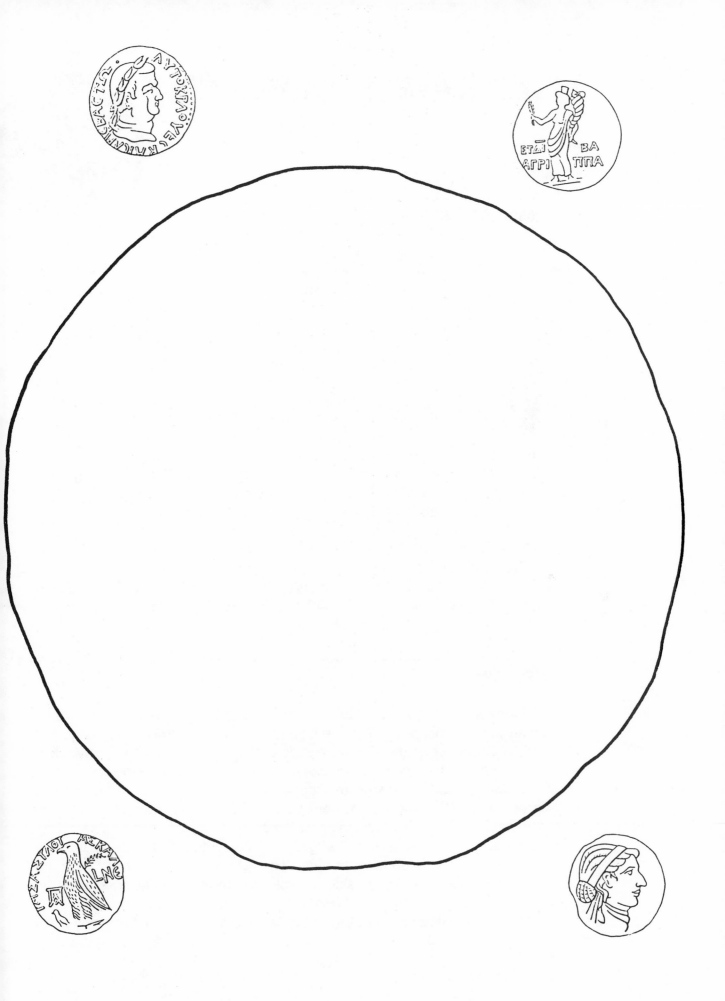

JERUSALEM: THE UPPER ROOM

Historical Notes

The day came during the Festival of Unleavened Bread when the lambs for the Passover meal were to be killed. Jesus sent Peter and John with these instructions: "Go and get the Passover meal ready for us to eat." (Luke 22:7-8)

Our celebration of the Lord's Supper has come down to us from the night when Jesus and his disciples shared the Passover meal in the upper room. When one examines the biblical accounts of this meal, various discoveries are made. For instance, all four Gospels tell the story, but John differs from Matthew, Mark, and Luke in setting the actual day of the week it took place. In addition, Jesus' words differ slightly in each account. Only Luke corresponds with Paul (I Corinthians 11:23-25) by quoting Jesus' words, "Do this in memory of me." Only Matthew adds that Jesus said "for the forgiveness of sins" during the distribution of the cup.

Following Jesus' ascension, this same upper room became the meeting room for the apostles (Acts 1:13). In A.D. 135, when Hadrian visited Jerusalem, a room called the Cenacle, on Mount Zion, was determined to be the actual upper room. Today in Jerusalem tourists still visit the Cenacle, but their imaginations, no doubt, feel much more at home with the vision of Leonardo da Vinci than with an empty stone room a short flight of steps above the "Upper Room Snack Bar"!

Tour Guide

Perhaps no other element of our current experience of worship draws us so close to the actual practice of Jesus and his disciples as the communion meal. When Christians gather around the table, they continue to use the words of Jesus in thankful remembrance of the past and hopeful anticipation of the future. Jesus' expression of love in that upper room has been a unifying force for generations of Christians, and it continues to be so as men, women, and children experience union with God and one another. Through the centuries, musicians, poets, and artists have been challenged to portray both what happened then and what happens now during that meal. The visions of Leonardo da Vinci and Salvador Dali stand side by side in depicting the majesty and mystery of the words, "Take, eat; this is my body."

For this crucial stop on our journey, we take the opportunity to look at the meal as it was then recorded, as it has been visually interpreted, and as it is now celebrated.

Itinerary

Jesus planned his arrival in Jerusalem for Sunday, when the city was crowded with people waiting to participate in the Passover observance.

On Thursday, Jesus celebrated the Passover meal with his disciples. They ate their meal in the upper room.

1. To understand what happened, read the story of this meal in Matthew 26:26-30, Mark 14:22-26, or Luke 22:14-20.

2. How was the Lord's Supper celebrated? In addition to authors who have written about the meal, artists have attempted to show this event in a picture. Look at the display of ways artists have interpreted the Lord's Supper. Then add your responses to the questions asked about some of the pictures.

3. How is the Lord's Supper celebrated in our church? Look closely at our communion utensils, the bulletin from our worship service, and the hymnal. Then answer these questions:
  —Who serves the communion meal?
  —When in the worship service is it served?
  —How is the congregation served?
  —What do the people do when they receive the elements?
  —What hymns are sung?

Jesus made preparations for the meal with his disciples. We also make preparations for our celebration of the Lord's Supper. We prepare ourselves; we pour the wine/grape juice; and we bake the bread.

4. Help make bread for our next communion meal. At that time, when we gather around the table, we will once again remember Jesus' meal with his disciples in the upper room.

5. Stamp your passport!

Setting the Scene

1. Post the itinerary.
2. Decorate the locale. Once again you have the opportunity to search the archives for a variety of visual representations of Jesus, this time as he hosts the Passover meal. As a part of the display, add questions and provide room for comments around some of the pictures. For instance, with Leonardo da Vinci's

"Last Supper" the questions "What did Jesus just say?" and "How are the disciples reacting?" can be posted. Any number of questions can be asked of Salvador Dali's "Last Supper"—for instance, "How do you feel when you look at this painting?" "What do you think the artist believes about communion?" Many artists depict Judas in a unique way. Others set the scene in their own culture. There is no lack of representations to add to the display.

Make sure copies of a Sunday communion service bulletin from your church are available, in addition to the communion utensils normally used.

The bread baking will take place most likely in the kitchen. You may wish to display some of the communion pictures in the bread baking area also. The easiest way to bake fresh bread is to buy frozen loaves at the grocery, defrost them, and *violà*! But purists will want to do everything from scratch. Certainly there is a bread expert in your congregation who would love to be a part of this locale.

3. Supply the locale.

> Checklist:
>   Bibles
>   Display of artists' interpretations of the Lord's Supper
>   Bulletins of a communion service
>   Set of communion utensils
>   Ingredients for baking bread

4. Set out passport stamp and stamp pad.

Jerusalem: Gethsemane

Historical Notes

>They came to a place called Gethsemane, and Jesus said to his disciples, "Sit here while I pray." (Mark 14:32)

Following their meal together, Jesus went with his disciples to the Mount of Olives, outside the walls of the city. At a site known as the Garden of Gethsemane, Jesus prayed while the disciples slept. All four Gospel writers tell the story of Jesus' prayers. Mark and Matthew identify the place as Gethsemane. Luke writes that it was "the place" on the mount of Olives where Jesus usually prayed. John is the one who describes it as a garden. The particular location, because it was a favorite place for Jesus, helped Judas know right where to lead the soldiers (John 18:2). Thus Gethsemane is also the scene of Jesus' betrayal and arrest.

The name *Gethsemane,* a Greek word from the Aramaic for "oil press," identifies the location as the site of an olive grove and olive press. Pilgrims who journey to the site today discover a beautiful, well-tended garden of eight ancient olive trees and many plants and flowers. In this peaceful setting, looking across the Kidron Valley to the walls of Jerusalem, one is easily able to imagine Jesus' choosing this setting to get away with his disciples for rest and prayer.

Tour Guide

Our visit to Gethsemane provides us the opportunity to focus on Jesus' life of prayer and his teachings about prayer. Throughout the Gospels, Jesus is known for his commitment to prayer. In fact, when you check out the concordance, you will discover that 99 percent of the references to prayer in the Gospels portray Jesus either praying or teaching his disciples how to pray.

Our activity in response to Jesus' life of prayer is assembling a journal—"Prayers on My Journey"—containing Jesus' teachings about prayer. The journal is designed to be used during the season of Lent. However, if you wish to make this journey and use this journal at another time of the year, simply change the weekly headings; the format is still appropriate.

Our activity in response to Jesus' invitation to pray is sharing written prayers on the Wall of Prayers.

Itinerary

After Jesus celebrated the Passover meal with his disciples, he went with them to the Garden of Gethsemane. From the Garden of Gethsemane, Jesus looked over the valley to the huge walls of Jerusalem.

1. Read the story in Mark 14:32-50. Jesus prayed. He prayed when he preached, when he taught, when he healed, when he ate with his friends, and when he prepared for death.

Jesus prayed by himself, and he prayed with others. In his life of prayer, Jesus was so at one with God that his friends asked, "Teach us to pray." Jesus taught them to pray.

2. Let us pray! *What is your prayer today?* On our wall of prayers are pictures, articles, names, and news stories that express joys, sorrows, concerns, and hopes. Meditate on each of these. Think about the people named and offer a prayer. Write your prayer on a slip of paper and add it to our wall of prayers. Even today, faithful Jews stuff written prayers in the cracks of the ancient Western Wall in Jerusalem.

3. Let us pray! *What are your prayers during this season?* Create a prayer journal to guide you on your journey. *Prayers on My Journey* expresses Jesus' teaching about prayer and suggests subjects for your life of prayer in these next seven weeks. Let it be a personal guide for you during this season of Lent, a season of prayer.

4. You may want to draw a picture on the cover. What picture comes to mind when you think of prayer? What do you see when you pray?

5. Stamp your passport!

Setting the Scene

The following directions and suggestions will help you put together the locale and set the scene as we follow Jesus to the Garden of Gethsemane.
1. Post the itinerary.
2. Decorate the locale. Since Gethsemane is a garden, you may wish to create a garden atmosphere using plants and flowers. In addition, consider displaying pictures of Jesus in prayer.

As the primary part of the locale, create a wall to provide a place for the travelers to post their own written prayers. Provide slips of paper in various colors and shapes for the travelers to use in writing their prayers. These can then be taped, glued, tacked, stapled, or attached in some way to the wall.

As a way to stimulate the prayers of the travelers, consider mounting items such as the following on the wall.

- Photographs
- Lists of college students, service personnel, home-bound members of the congregation
- Pages from the newspaper
- News magazine stories
- Church newsletter articles
- Pages from the church directory
- Pages from the Mission Yearbook for Prayer and Study

3. Supply the locale. Reproduce sufficient copies of each of the pages of *Prayers on My Journey,* on the following pages, for the travelers to put together.

Checklist:
Bibles
Pieces of paper for the written prayers
Pencils, pens, crayons, and so on
The pages of *Prayers on My Journey,* photocopied in sufficient quantity
Stapler, staples

4. Set out passport stamp and stamp pad.

PRAYERS ON MY JOURNEY

Ash Wednesday

"But when you pray, go to your room, close the door, and pray to your Father, who is unseen. And your Father, who sees what you do in private, will reward you."

Matthew 6:6

Today as I begin to pray, these are my thoughts and feelings about prayer . . .

The specific concerns I pray about today are . . .

The First Week in Lent

Our Father who art in heaven,
Hallowed be thy name.
Thy kingdom come,
Thy will be done,
   On earth as it is in heaven.
Give us this day our daily bread;
And forgive us our debts,
   As we also have forgiven our
     debtors;
And lead us not into temptation,
   But deliver us from evil.

Matthew 6:9 (RSV)

As I pray our Lord's prayer, I remember those who are sick and those who sorrow.

This week my prayers for our world are . . .

The Second Week In Lent

You have heard that it was said, "Love your friends, hate your enemies." But now I tell you: love your enemies and pray for those who persecute you, so that you may become the sons of your Father in heaven.

Matthew 5:43

As I hear and understand Jesus' words, the following people come to mind for my prayers this week . . .

This week my specific concerns for myself are . . .

The Third Week in Lent

And when you stand and pray, forgive anything you may have against anyone, so that your Father in heaven will forgive the wrongs you have done.

Mark 11:25

This week as I am praying, I will forgive . . .

This week as I am praying, I will seek the forgiveness of . . .

The Fourth Week in Lent

I pray not only for them, but also for those who believe in me because of their message. I pray that they may all be one. Father! May they be in us, just as you are in me and I am in you. May they be one, so that the world will believe that you sent me.

John 17:20-21

This week as I consider Jesus' prayer for unity, I will express the following feelings and hopes in my prayers . . .

Some specific concerns for unity are directed to . . .

The Fifth Week in Lent

Jesus went into the Temple and drove out all those who were buying and selling there. He overturned the tables of the moneychangers and the stools of those who sold pigeons, and said to them, "It is written in the Scriptures that God said, 'My Temple will be called a house of prayer.' But you are making it a hideout for thieves!"

Matthew 21:12-13

This week I pray for the Church. My prayers about my church concern . . .

When I consider the worldwide Church, my prayers focus on . . .

The Sixth Week in Lent

". . . How is it that you three were not able to keep watch with me for even one hour? Keep watch and pray that you will not fall into temptation. The spirit is willing, but the flesh is weak."

Matthew 26:40-41

This week will be a time when I ask for strength in my weakness. I need to pray about . . .

In journeying with Jesus in Jerusalem, I reflect on his experiences in my prayers. Our loving God, I pray that . . .

Easter

Be joyful always, pray at all times, be thankful in all circumstances. This is what God wants from you in your life in union with Christ Jesus.

I Thessalonians 5:16-18

Today I rejoice! My prayers especially reflect the joy I have found in . . .

To celebrate the new life, I give thanks—in all circumstances! Most gracious and loving God, I give thanks for . . .

Easter Week

In the same way the Spirit also comes to help us, weak as we are. For we do not know how we ought to pray; the Spirit himself pleads with God for us in groans that words cannot express.

Romans 8:26

This is a week to listen to the Holy Spirit. As I listen, I hear and feel . . .

As the Spirit intercedes so also do I offer prayers of intercession for . . .

JERUSALEM: GOLGOTHA

Historical Notes

> Then Pilate handed Jesus over to them to be crucified.
>
> So they took charge of Jesus. He went out, carrying his cross, and came to "The place of the Skull," as it is called. (In Hebrew it is called "Golgotha.") There they crucified him; and they also crucified two other men, one on each side, with Jesus between them. (John 19:16-18)

Golgotha was located outside the walls of Jerusalem. The origin of its name is unknown, but the basic word translates "skull." In Hebrew, the word is *Golgotha,* in Greek it is *Cranium,* and in Latin it is *Calvary.*

Jesus was put to death at Golgotha, the "Place of the Skull." Did the rock formation look like a skull? Were skulls from previous executions lying around? A popular medieval theme is the early Christian legend that Jesus' cross was placed directly over Adam's skull.

As with most of the sacred sites, it has been impossible to determine the exact location of Golgotha within modern Jerusalem. The Church of the Holy Sepulchre has traditionally been identified as the site of Jesus' death, burial, and resurrection. Yet accretions on the church over the centuries challenge the traveler to imagine that site as the actual location. Those who support the authenticity of the Garden Tomb as the true site have convincing evidence—the rock around this tomb *is* shaped like a skull!

Tour Guide

The powerful central image of our faith is the central image of this locale. Yet even though the cross is widely used today on everything imaginable, it was not always so. The cross began to be used in Christian art four hundred years after Jesus' death. Until that time, it was seen as shameful, scandalous, and evidence of a criminal's death. Other images, such as Jesus the Good Shepherd and Jesus the host at communion, were understood to be more edifying and positive—especially since the Church was seeking new members!

Golgotha provides us an opportunity to see how central the cross has become over the centuries and how important the cross is within our particular church.

The other visual image for this locale is that of a seed. Jesus and Paul both expressed the mystery of the resurrected life by using the symbol of a seed, planted in the earth and growing in a new form.

83

Itinerary

On Friday, Jesus carried his cross outside the city to Golgotha, the place of the skull. There he died—nailed upon a cross.

1. Read John 19:17-20 for the story of Jesus' crucifixion. The cross is the most important symbol of the Christian faith. Look at the display of crosses that have been designed and used within the Christian Church over the centuries.

2. Continue your journey by taking a discovery tour in your church building. Take along the pages of twelve crosses and see which ones you can find. Look especially in the sanctuary to discover how many crosses we have there to remind us of God's love when we worship. Return here when your tour is over.

Jesus' cross is empty! The cross continually reminds us of God's great love in raising Jesus to new life. We are Easter people and know that Jesus did not remain on the cross but rose to new life!

Jesus and Paul both help us understand this new life by teaching about seeds.

3. Read either John 12:23-25 or I Corinthians 15:35-38. Then plant a kernel of wheat in a cup. Water it and take it home with you. It will take some time for it to grow. When it does sprout, remember Jesus' teaching about the seed and give thanks to God for new life and the hope of Easter!

4. Stamp your passport!

Setting the Scene

The following directions should help you put together the locale and set the scene as we gather around Jesus' cross on Golgotha.

1. Post the itinerary.

2. Decorate the locale. In contrast to many of the other locales, Golgotha should be kept simple, even rather stark. Focus attention on the display of crosses.

3. Supply the locale. Reproduce sufficient quantities of the two pages of crosses for each of the travelers to have copies. Buy seeds that are fast growing.

Checklist:
    Bibles
    Cross display using either pictures of the twelve crosses in this book or
        actual crosses
    Paper, pencils "for Discovery Tour"
    Plastic cups
    Potting soil
    Seeds (any fast growing grain or bean)
    Water

4. Set out passport stamp and stamp pad.

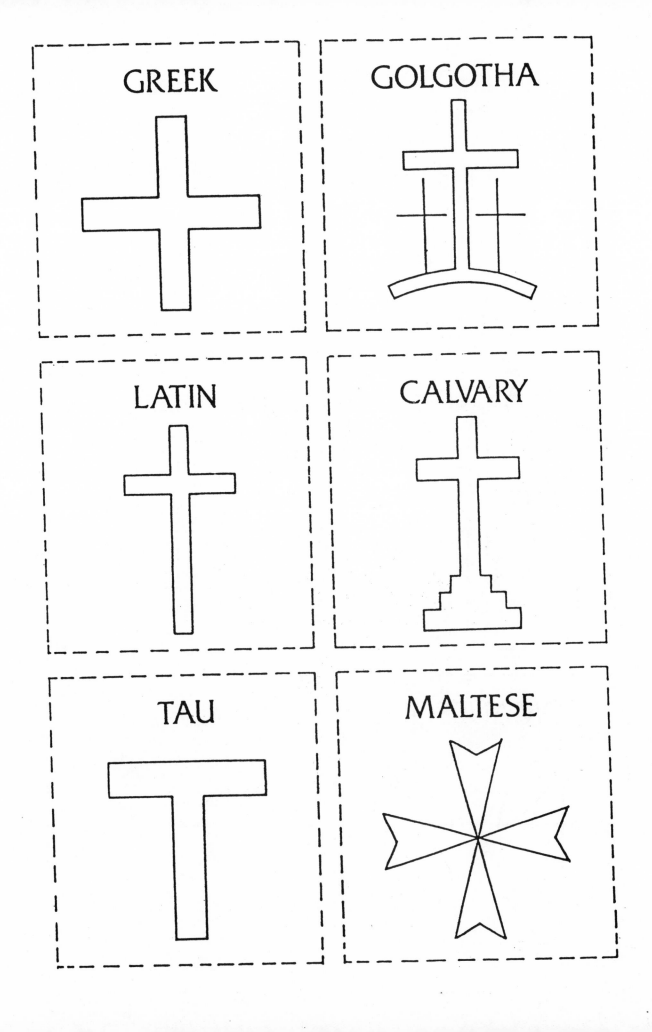

GREEK

GOLGOTHA

LATIN

CALVARY

TAU

MALTESE

ANCHOR

CELTIC

EASTERN

JERUSALEM

ROMANESQUE

ST. ANDREW'S

JERUSALEM: THE EMPTY TOMB

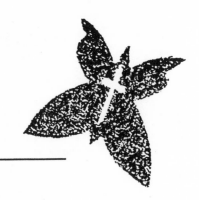

Historical Notes

> Very early on Sunday morning the women went to the tomb, carrying the spices they had prepared. They found the stone rolled away from the entrance to the tomb, so they went in; but they did not find the body of the Lord Jesus. (Luke 24:1-3)

We know little about Jesus' tomb other than that it belonged to Joseph of Arimathea, whom Luke described as "a good and honorable man, who was waiting for the coming of the Kingdom of God" (Luke 23:50). It was a new tomb, unused and located in a garden (John 19:41); it was sealed by a large round stone, and it was large enough for the disciples to enter (Luke 24:2-3).

Today, two sites vie for designation as Jesus' tomb. From the fourth century on, the Church of the Holy Sepulchre has been thought to stand on the sites of Golgotha and the entombment. Before its construction, there was little interest in identifying the exact location of the tomb. In 1867, another site, was put forward by the English adventurer General Charles George Gordon as the true place of Jesus' entombment. That site, identified as Gordon's Calvary or the Garden Tomb, is also visited by today's pilgrims.

Tour Guide

It matters little that we can with certainty locate the tomb. It is not the empty tomb, but rather the personal encounters with the risen Christ that give evidence of the resurrection. Just as there is no single story of Jesus' birth, so also there is no single story of his resurrection. Each of the Gospels shares personal experiences with the crucified and risen Christ. In order to discover this theme in the Gospel records, our focus at this locale is a close look at those records. Then, in order to express our own Easter experiences, the travelers are invited to decorate a butterfly—a symbol of the resurrection—with expressions of new life and signs of hope.

Christ is risen!
He is risen indeed!

We are now at the end/beginning of our journey to discover that Easter means experiencing the living Christ. What did the disciples experience on Easter?

1. Read two or more of the following stories of Jesus' resurrection:

- Matthew 28:1-10
- Mark 16:1-8
- Luke 24:1-10
- John 20:1-10

Then use the printed form "Easter Is Experiencing the Risen Christ" and answer the three questions:

—Who went to the tomb?
—What did they see there?
—Who did they tell?

You may want to read and compare all four experiences with the risen Christ. Each one expresses the wonderful event through different eyes. Easter is experiencing the risen Christ.

2. What is your experience of Easter? Share with those on the journey by writing or drawing on a paper butterfly. The butterfly, because of its transformation, is one of many symbols of resurrection—a symbol of the risen Christ.

Share your expressions of
—new life
　—new hope
　　—new joys
　　　—new dreams
　　　　—and a new future

May each of us celebrate Easter by experiencing the living Christ in our lives! Add your butterfly to the locale so that others may see Easter through your eyes.

Christ is risen!
He is risen indeed!

88　　**3.** Stamp your passport!

Setting the Scene

The following directions and suggestions will help you put together the locale and set the scene as we approach with wonder the empty tomb.

1. Post the itinerary.

2. Decorate the locale. Once again it is possible to decorate the locale by using artists' renditions of Easter. But as you will discover, reproductions of this event are more difficult to find, and the images are diverse. Perhaps that diversity will underscore the theme of the locale, the variety of personal experiences with Jesus Christ.

Create an easy way to hang the butterflies at the locale once they have been completed.

3. Supply the locale. Reproduce sufficient quantities of the printed form "Easter Is Experiencing the Risen Christ" and the butterfly pattern.

Checklist:
Bibles
Printed form with questions
Butterflies to cut out
Scissors
Pencils, pens, crayons, and so on
Yarn and so on for flying the butterflies

4. Set out passport stamp and stamp pad.

Easter Is Experiencing The Risen Christ

	Matt:28:1-10	Mark 16:1-8	Luke 24:1-10	John 20:1-10
Who went to the tomb?				
Who did they see there?				
Who did they tell?				

EMMAUS

Historical Notes

On that same day two of Jesus' followers were going to a village named Emmaus, about seven miles from Jerusalem, and they were talking to each other about all the things that had happened. As they talked and discussed, Jesus himself drew near and walked along with them. (Luke 24:13-15)

This is the only mention of Emmaus in our Bible, although it is noted twice in the Apocryphal book of I Maccabees. According to Luke, the only author to include this story in his Gospel, Emmaus was a village seven miles from Jerusalem. Today four different villages in Israel claim to be ancient Emmaus, and they range in distance from four to twenty miles from Jerusalem. We will never be certain about the authentic one. Yet, even with a solitary mention, Emmaus is a crucial locale because of Jesus' Easter day appearance when "he was known to them in the breaking of bread."

Tour Guide

Luke's story of the walk to Emmaus ends with the disciple's exclamation, "Wasn't it like a fire burning in us when he talked to us on the road and explained the Scriptures to us?" (Luke 24:32). In opening the scriptures and breaking the bread, Jesus was indicating the way he would continue to reveal himself to the disciples.

One vivid way that the scriptures come alive for us today is through music. Most of our hymns and anthems are inspired by the words of scripture. In fact, the hymn "Abide with Me" was inspired by this very story and the words "But they constrained him, saying, Abide with us; for it is toward evening and the day is far spent" (Luke 24:29 KJV). Music has the power to cause intense emotions and even create some burning fires within us. Therefore, Easter expressed in song is the focus for our visit to Emmaus. Many possibilities exist for incorporating both familiar and new Easter songs at this locale.

Itinerary

Have you heard the good news? The Lord has risen indeed! He has joined us on the road to Emmaus.

1. Read the story in Luke 24:13-35. When the travelers realized that it was Jesus with them on the journey, they immediately returned to Jerusalem to share the good news with the disciples. Their message was something to sing about! The Lord has risen! The Lord had risen indeed!

2. Let us express our joy by sharing together the good news of Easter in song. As we sing, let us remember the way Jesus explained the scriptures when the disciples described it as "a fire burning within us." Join _____ in singing the message of Easter in songs both familiar and new. Let us express joy in Jesus' resurrection by letting the expressions of hope found in scripture burn within us.

The selections are:
  "Jesus Christ Is Risen Today"
  "The Day of Resurrection"
  "Allelu"
  "I Am the Resurrection"
  "Lord of the Dance"
  "Christ the Lord Is Risen Today"
  "Every Morning Is Easter Morning"
  "Good News Is Ours to Tell"
  "Christ on the Cross Our Life Has Bought"
  "Jesus Christ, Whose Passion Claims Us"

Emmaus is the final stop on our journey. Yet, as the disciples discovered, the journey was just beginning. Grace and peace as you continue your journey of faith.

Setting the Scene

The following directions and suggestions will help you put together the locale and set the scene as we join Jesus on the road to Emmaus.
1. Post the itinerary.
2. Decorate the locale. Since the music may be too loud for the main room, Emmaus would benefit by being located in a setting away from the rest of the journey. Obviously you will need a room with a piano, or other instrument, and good acoustics. Enlist a song leader for the locale who will be comfortable gathering an informal group of travelers together for singing. The atmosphere should be one of Easter caroling. Encourage the song leader to highlight the way scripture has been used in the songs.

In considering ways to decorate this locale, think about the way you would decorate for a joyous party: balloons, streamers, party hats, confetti! Why not?

One suggestion for concluding the entire experience of "Journey to Jerusalem" is to share Emmaus as a total group. Gather the travelers together in the sanctuary for a reading of the Emmaus road story and a grand songfest of Easter music, or gather the travelers together in the central room of the journey and use the locales to review the journey.

An alternative idea for this locale, if live music is not possible, is to pre-record all the music on either a cassette or a videotape. The music could then be shared at the locale by using either earphones and tape recorder or television monitor and videotape. Consider the possibility of making a recording or videotape of your own adult and children's choirs singing Easter music. It would certainly provide a personal touch for the visit to Emmaus.

3. Supply the locale. Remember copyright laws when you make your song sheets for this locale! You may wish to write the words on a transparency and use an overhead projector. The composers and sources for suggested songs follow. You may want to adjust the list to include favorites from your church's hymnal and collection of music.

Suggested titles:
"Jesus Christ Is Risen Today" (tune "Easter Hymn," Hymnal)
"Christ the Lord Is Risen Today" (tune "Llanfair," Hymnal)
"The Day of Resurrection" (tune "Lancashire," Hymnal)
"Allelu" (Ray Repp, *Hymnal for Young Christians*)
"I Am the Resurrection" (Ray Repp, *Hymnal for Young Christians*)
"Lord of the Dance" (Shaker tune, words Sydney Carter, Hymnal)
"Every Morning Is Easter Morning" (Richard Avery and Donald Marsh, *Hymns Hot and Carols Cool*)
"Good News Is Ours to Tell" (tune "Festal Song," words Jane Parker Huber, *Creation Sings*)
"Christ on the Cross Our Life Has Bought" (tune "Quebec," words Jane Parker Huber, *Joy in Singing*)
"Jesus Christ, Whose Passion Claims Us" (tune "Lord, Revive Us," words Jane Parker Huber, *Joy in Singing*)

Checklist:
Bibles
Song leader
Piano, guitar
Hymnals, songbooks, or song sheets
Transparencies, overhead projector
Tape recorder and cassette tape
Videotape and television monitor

4. Set out passport stamp and stamp pad.

Baggage Checklist

Bethlehem
Bibles
"Jesus' Family Tree" form for each traveler
Pencils, pens
Bible dictionaries, name dictionaries

Nazareth: Jesus the Child
Bibles
Yoke display—pictures and so on
Scraps of wood in all shapes and sizes
Nails, hammers, saws
White glue
Supplies for wooden crosses
    3″ pieces of ¼″ balsa wood
    1″ pieces of ¼″ balsa wood
    lengths of macrame cord to make necklace
    hand drill with a small bit (but large enough to get the cord through)

The Jordan River
Bibles
Squares of felt in various colors
Other felt—large pieces, scraps, and so on
Yarn, ribbon
White glue
Pencils
Scissors

Nazareth: Jesus Begins His Ministry
Bibles
Stick for scrolls (look for craft sticks in an art or hobby shop)
Long sheets of paper for scrolls
Hebrew/English phrases to copy
Pencils, crayons, marking pens, glue

The Sea of Galilee
Bibles

Copies of the fish stained-glass window
Paper frames for the window (cut these out beforehand)
Crayons, liquid markers
Vegetable oil
Paper towels
Tape, staples, and stapler for securing the paper frame

Bethsaida
Bibles
Arch filmstrip *The Boy Who Gave His Lunch Away*
Copies of the Arch book of the same title
Filmstrip projector
Record player
Copies of illumination of Matthew 25
Paint pens, marking pens, and so on
Hunger program materials (optional)

Capernaum
Bibles
Copies of "Capernaum Interview Form"
Clipboards
Pencils, pens

Caesarea Philippi
Bibles
A display of portraits of Jesus
Pencils, markers, brushes, paint, clay, and so on for visual expression
Paper for written responses to pictures
Paper for "I believe" statements

Jericho
Bibles

Materials for the greeting cards—
paint, tissue paper, glue, rubber
stamps, potato prints, stickers,
and so on (provide variety!)
Envelopes, postage stamps
Display of "Neighbors"

Bethany
Bibles
Wall room divider, board with eight
hooks, or table with eight days
of the week indicated
Eight pictures/paintings of Jesus
during Holy Week
Copies of the "Holy Week Puzzle"
(colored background sheet and
white puzzle-piece sheet)
Scissors
Glue
Crayons, colored pencils, marking
pens, and so on

Jerusalem: The Temple
Bibles
Materials for coin display
Coin patterns
Pencils, marking pens, and so on for
designing coins
Film *Show-Off* (this Story Line film
may be purchased or rented
from the American Bible So-
ciety 1865 Broadway, New
York, NY 10023)
Film projector

Jerusalem: The Upper Room
Bibles
Display of artists' interpretations of
the Lord's Supper
Bulletins of a communion service
Set of communion utensils

Ingredients for baking bread

Jerusalem: Gethsemane
Bibles
Pieces of paper for the written
prayers
Pencils, pens, crayons, and so on
The pages of *Prayers on My Journey*
photocopied in sufficient quan-
tity
Stapler, staples

Jerusalem: Golgotha
Bibles
Cross display using either pictures of
the twelve crosses in this book
or actual crosses
Paper, pencils for "Discovery Tour"
Plastic cups
Potting soil
Wheat (or any fast growing grain or
bean)
Water

Jerusalem: The Empty Tomb
Bibles
Printed form with questions
Butterflies to cut out
Scissors
Pencils, pens, crayons, and so on
Yarn and so on for flying the
butterflies

Emmaus
Bibles
Song leader
Piano, guitar
Hymnals, songbooks, or song
sheets
Transparencies, overhead projector
Tape recorder and cassette tape
Videotape and television monitor